Money and number

The School Mathematics Project

CAMBRIDGE
UNIVERSITY PRESS

Main authors   Stan Dolan
                   Ron Haydock
                   Paul Roder

Team leader   Stan Dolan

The authors and publishers are grateful to:

Miles Barton and *The Times Educational Supplement* for permission to reproduce the extract on page 18;
National Savings for permission to reproduce the extract on page 51;
Bank of Scotland for permission to reproduce the extract on page 58;
The Controller of Her Majesty's Stationery Office for permission to reproduce the extract on page 55;
British Rail for permission to reproduce the extracts on pages 59 and 60;
British Gas PLC for permission to reproduce the extract on page 62.

The authors and publishers would like to thank the following for supplying photographs:

cover – Market day, Fakenham Norfolk, Robert Harding Picture Library;
page 2 (bacterium) – Dr Tony Braine/Science Photo Library;
page 2 (child) – ZEFA Picture Library (UK) Ltd;
page 2 (UK) – NRSC Ltd/Science Photo Library;
page 2 (Jupiter) – Space Telescope Science Institute/NASA/Science Photo Library;
page 58 – NASA/Science Photo Library.

Published by the Press Syndicate of the University of Cambridge
The Pitt Building, Trumpington Street, Cambridge CB2 1RP
40 West 20th Street, New York, NY 10011–4211, USA
10 Stamford Road, Oakleigh, Melbourne 3166, Australia

© Cambridge University Press 1993

First published 1993

Produced by Gecko Limited, Bicester, Oxon

Cover design by Iguana Creative Design

Printed in Great Britain by Scotprint Ltd, Musselburgh

Library of Congress cataloguing in publication data applied for

A catalogue record for this book is available from the British Library

ISBN 0 521 44733 X

Contents

1 The world of work

1.1 Piece-rates

One of the most straightforward ways of being paid for work is by the piece. You are paid a certain amount for each accepted item which you produce.

(a) Strawberry pickers are paid at the rate of 17p per punnet. How much would be paid for 100 punnets?

(b) A picker hands in 153 punnets, of which eleven are rejected. How much does the picker receive?

(c) A picker decides to set a target of £40 per day. How many punnets must she fill to achieve this?

(d) Apart from piece-work, what other ways are there of being paid for your work? Think of as many different ways as you can. What are the advantages and disadvantages of each method of payment for the employee and employer?

A combination of basic pay and various forms of piece-rate is more common than paying a piece-work rate only.

EXAMPLE 1

A checker in a light engineering firm receives basic pay of £134 per week. He also receives a piece-work rate of £2·15 per thousand components checked.

In one week his output is as follows.

Day	1	2	3	4	5
Output	5200	4700	4500	4800	4200

What is his pay for the week's work?

SOLUTION

The number of components checked is:

$$5200 + 4700 + 4500 + 4800 + 4200 = 23\,400.$$

The piece-work pay is $23.4 \times £2.15 = £50.31$.
The total pay is $£134 + £50.31 = £184.31$.

EXERCISE 1

1 A market researcher is conducting a survey on shopping habits. She is paid 84p for every interview with a shopper. In a morning's work she interviews 53 shoppers. How much has she earned?

2 Mrs Price works at home addressing envelopes. The rate of pay is £6·30 per hundred envelopes.

(a) What is her rate per thousand envelopes?

(b) In a week she addresses 2200 envelopes. How much is she paid?

3 Ali hand-finishes shoes. He has a basic wage of £42 per week, on top of which he earns £1·60 per pair for the first ten pairs of shoes he finishes each day and £3·20 per pair for any extra pairs. Calculate his pay for a week in which his daily output on successive days in pairs of shoes is 13, 9, 8, 12 and 14.

4 In a unit which produces kitchen stools the shop-floor workers are given the choice between two methods of payment:

Method A: Basic wage £64 per week + £2·60 per stool

Method B: Straight piece-work at £4·30 per stool

If each worker averages 48 stools per week, which method of payment should the workers choose?

5 An egg-packing firm pays its workers a basic wage of £116 for a 5-day week. A daily quota of 1500 boxes is set – any additional boxes packed earn 12p for every ten. One week Margaret exceeds the quota every day and packs a total of 10 220 boxes. How much does she earn?

1.2 **Time-rates**

Many employees work for a fixed number of hours per week and are paid a fixed sum for their time. When the payment is made weekly it is normally called a wage; when it is paid monthly it is called a salary.

(a) Maria is a computer operator. She works a 36-hour week and her hourly rate is £8·24. What is her monthly salary? (Assume that there are precisely 52 weeks in a year.)

(b) Andrew works a 38-hour week for which his pay is £126·92. What is his hourly rate?

An increasingly popular working arrangement is flexitime. The weekly number of hours is fixed but the employee is allowed some choice in the times of clocking in and clocking out.

Maria's times of clocking in and out in a particular week are as follows:

Day	In	Out	In	Out
Monday	09:30	13:00	13:45	16:45
Tuesday	08:45	12:45	13:15	16:45
Wednesday	09:00	12:45	13:30	16:45
Thursday	09:15	13:00	14:00	16:30
Friday	08:45	12:45	13:15	

At what time must she clock out on Friday afternoon if she is to complete her 36 hours?

Employees on time-rates may often need to work more than the basic number of hours. Such overtime is often paid at higher rates – time and a half or double time are sometimes used.

> Double time can be thought of in two different ways:
>
> - 1 hour at double time earns the same as 2 hours at standard rate;
>
> - the rate paid on double time is twice the standard rate.

E X A M P L E 2

Mr Singh works a basic 36-hour week at an hourly rate of £6·14. One week he does overtime – 3 hours at time and a half and 4 hours at double time. What is his pay for the week?

S O L U T I O N

Basic:	$36 \times £6·14 = £221·04$
Time and a half:	$3 \times (1·5 \times £6·14) = £27·63$
Double time:	$4 \times (2 \times £6·14) = £49·12$
Total pay:	£297·79

T A S K S H E E T 1 – A working week (page 14)

Whether working on piece-rates or on time-rates, an increasing number of people, especially those with young children, have part-time jobs. Sometimes a person working part-time shares a full-time job with another person.

Many factories operate 24 hours every day, 7 days a week, to keep production going. To achieve this the working day is divided into shifts. There may, for instance, be a morning shift, an afternoon shift and a night shift. Workers on the night shift are often paid at a higher overtime rate.

EXERCISE 2

1   A lathe operator earns a basic rate of £5·24 per hour and is paid time and a half for the night shift. Find her wage for a week in which she does 8 hours on a day shift at the basic rate and 32 hours on the night shift.

2   Jack works for a firm of builders. His basic rate of pay is £4·26 per hour for a 38-hour week, finishing at 5 p.m. daily, Monday to Friday. Any time worked after 5 p.m. or on Saturday is paid at time and a half, whilst work on Sundays is paid at double time. On a rushed job he is working until 7 p.m. every weekday and does 4 hours on Saturday and again on Sunday. What is his weekly wage?

3   Leila works flexitime. She has to work 36 hours per week and, so that she can leave early on Friday, she usually works longer on the other four days. On Monday to Thursday she clocks in at 9 a.m., takes 45 minutes for lunch and clocks out at 5:30 p.m. On Friday she follows the same pattern except that her clocking out time is earlier. What time is it?

4

(a)   The basic weekly wage for a weaver in a cotton mill is £157·70 for a 38-hour week. What is the basic hourly rate?

(b)   Gopal works at the mill and in a particular week his pay is £207·50, including overtime pay at time and a half. How much overtime has he worked?

1.3 Commission

Employees responsible for selling goods, whether as shop assistants or travelling sales people, often earn commission on their sales. This takes the form of a percentage of the value of the goods sold. A basic wage or salary may be paid in addition to the commission.

EXAMPLE 3

A car salesman earns a basic salary of £720 a month. In addition he is awarded commission of 5% on any sales after the first £10000. What is his salary in a month in which he secures sales of £15 400?

SOLUTION

His sales above the first £10000 are £(15 400 − 10000) = £5400.
His commission is 5% of £5400 = 0·05 × £5400 = £270.
His salary is £720 + £270 = £990.

Percentages will be studied in more detail in later chapters. For now it is sufficient to know the following.

> - To find 1% of a quantity, multiply it by 0·01;
> - to find 5% of a quantity, multiply it by 0·05;
> - to find 10% of a quantity, multiply it by 0·10;
> and so on.

EXERCISE 3

1 An animal feed salesman has a basic salary of £850 per month and earns commission at the rate of 10% on all sales. What is his salary for a month in which his sales total £13 400?

2

£92 400 £105 500 £72 800

An estate agent charges commission at two rates, 2% on the first £50 000 of the sale price of the house and 1% on the remainder. What is her commission on each of the houses shown?

3 Trish has the offer of two jobs. Job A offers a basic salary of £540 a month and 2% commission on sales over £1000. She can expect to average sales of £4500 per month. However, she will have to pay £180 a month for her child to be cared for. Job B pays a straight wage of £120 per week but offers free crèche facilities. Which job is better financially?

4

DoubleSURE
weather-proofing
Representative needed:
salary £5200 p.a., company car,
5% commission on all sales.
Likely sales in a year are £100 000.

Winterwarm double-glazing
Representatives required:
salary £7500 p.a., 4%
commission on all sales over
£50 000. You can expect sales
to average £200 000.

(a) Assuming that the company car is worth £2300 per year, how much can you expect to earn in a year working for Doublesure?
How much are you likely to earn in a year working for Winterwarm?
Which job would you choose? Why?

(b) What sales would the Winterwarm representative have to make to achieve a gross salary of £20 000?

1.4 Self-employment

Self-employed people follow many occupations. These include free-lance journalism, market trading, lorry driving and acting.

> What are the advantages and disadvantages of being self-employed?

Some self-employed people earn agreed fees for specific jobs for which they make a contract with an employer. This may take the form of a written quotation or simply a verbal agreement (for example between a householder and a plumber) or can involve the signing of a legally-binding agreement.

E X A M P L E 4

Mr Patel is a self-employed electrician. He has made notes on a job for Mrs Simpson.

○
○
○
○

4 × thirteen-amp outlets @ £4·75 per outlet
fuse box £8·25
25 m of cable @ 42p per m
sundries £5
Allow for labour: 8 hrs @ £6·80 per hr

What would his quotation look like?

S O L U T I O N

He first calculates the total cost of the job:

$$£19 + £8·25 + £10·50 + £5 + £54·40 = £97·15$$

The quotation might then be made on Mr Patel's business writing paper.

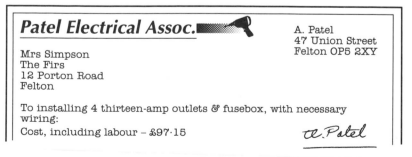

Patel Electrical Assoc.

A. Patel
47 Union Street
Felton OP5 2XY

Mrs Simpson
The Firs
12 Porton Road
Felton

To installing 4 thirteen-amp outlets & fusebox, with necessary wiring:
Cost, including labour – £97·15

A. Patel

A self-employed person takes his or her income out of the profits from the business. At the end of the financial year accounts must be prepared for tax purposes.

T A S K S H E E T   2E   –   Preparing accounts (page 15)

An important item on many business accounts is **depreciation**. Many assets owned by the business will be used for many years, gradually losing value over this period of time. This depreciation is considered as a business expense.

E X A M P L E   5

Jim is a self-employed printer who has just bought a new photocopier for his business. It cost him £8400. He is advised that depreciation in the first year will be 20%. By how much does this depreciation increase his operating expenses?

S O L U T I O N

20% of £8400 = 0·2 × £8400
= £1680

E X E R C I S E   4

1 A fencing contractor makes notes for a job as follows:

> netting: 460 m @ £36 per 100 m roll
> standard posts: 230 @ £1·50
> corner posts: 18 @ £4·20 each
> staples etc: £3·40
> labour: 12 hours @ £7·50 per hour

What is the total amount of his quotation for the job?

2 A lorry driver starts the year with a new vehicle costing £48000. Her accountant estimates that it depreciates in value at the rate of 10% per year. The annual cost of maintenance is £1400 and fuel costs £2300. What is the total of the expenses for the lorry for the year?

3E Mr Sanchez works as a translator from a small office which he rents at £560 per month. The electricity bill for the office averages £140 per quarter. His other business expenses for the year are as follows.

> Telephone £420
> Postage £780
> Stationery and printing £680

If his fees total £29 460 prepare his profit and loss account, assuming he takes all the operating profit as salary.

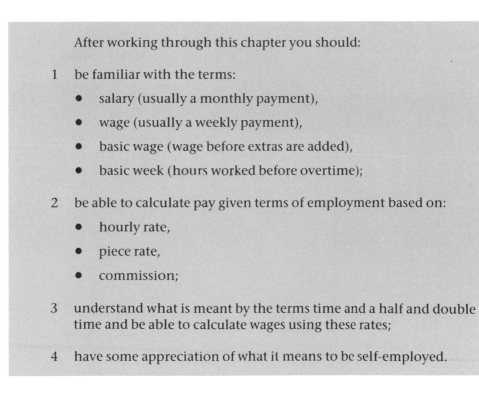

After working through this chapter you should:

1   be familiar with the terms:

- salary (usually a monthly payment),

- wage (usually a weekly payment),

- basic wage (wage before extras are added),

- basic week (hours worked before overtime);

2   be able to calculate pay given terms of employment based on:

- hourly rate,

- piece rate,

- commission;

3   understand what is meant by the terms time and a half and double time and be able to calculate wages using these rates;

4   have some appreciation of what it means to be self-employed.

A working week

Mrs Turner works as a finisher for the Bestsox hosiery firm. Her basic working week is 36 hours and her basic rate of pay is £4·48 per hour. Any hours over the basic 36 are paid at time and a half. In one particular week she clocks in and out on every day from Monday to Friday inclusive as shown in the table.

Time (hours)	In	Out	In	Out
	08:00	12:30	13:15	17:15

1 How many hours does she work:

(a) each day,

(b) in the whole week?

2 What is Mrs Turner's basic pay for a 36-hour week?

3 How much is she paid for this particular week?

The firm has a bonus scheme for finishers. Those with an output of more than 80 pairs of socks per hour earn 5p per pair for each pair in excess of 80. Mrs Turner consistently finishes 92 pairs per hour.

4 What is Mrs Turner's gross pay for the week?

[Gross pay is the pay before various deductions such as National Insurance, income tax and pension contributions are made. Some of these deductions are studied in chapter 4.]

Preparing accounts

Mrs Leroy is a self-employed cabinet maker with a small workshop and van. Her profit and loss account for the financial year 1992–3 is as shown.

Profit and loss account

	£	£
Total sales		35 300
Cost of goods sold		11 800
Gross profit		23 500

Less operating expenses

	£	£
Rent, rates	600	
Light and heat	430	
Van expenses	1730	
Advertising and sundries	680	3 440
Operating profit		20 060
Less salary		15 000
Retained profits		5 060

Notes

- The first three lines of the account show that Mrs Leroy sold goods for £35 300, whereas the materials had cost her only £11 800. The difference of £23 500 is her gross profit.

- Mrs Leroy will have had many expenses. These are listed in the second section of the accounts and total £3440. This is deducted from the gross profit to give the operating profit of £20 060.

- Finally, Mrs Leroy has to take her salary out of the profits. This leaves £5060 which can be kept in the business, perhaps to be invested in more equipment.

1 Mrs Leroy has a friend called Mr Burgin who keeps a corner shop. The total sales for 1992–3 were £49 360 and the cost of the goods sold was £25 020.

What was Mr Burgin's gross profit?

2 Mr Burgin has kept records of all his expenses on various slips of paper.
Find his total operating expenses.

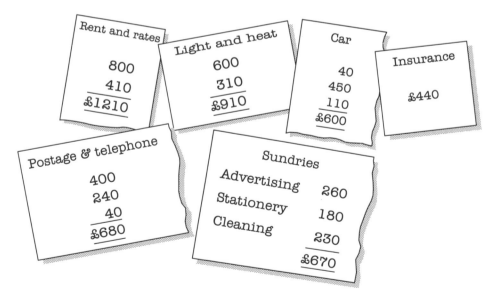

Rent and rates

800
410
————
£1210

Light and heat

600
310
————
£910

Car

40
450
110
————
£600

Insurance

£440

Postage & telephone

400
240
40
————
£680

Sundries

Advertising   260
Stationery   180
Cleaning   230
                ————
                £670

3 Mr Burgin retains 10% of his operating profit in the business and takes the rest as salary. Draw up a profit and loss account for the year.

Using numbers

2.1 Representing numbers

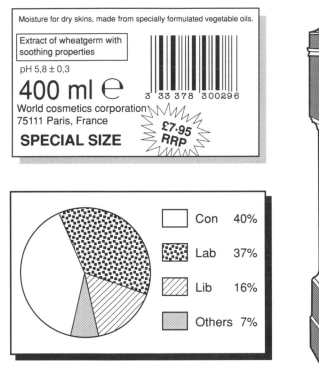

Moisture for dry skins, made from specially formulated vegetable oils.

Extract of wheatgerm with soothing properties

pH 5,8 ± 0,3

400 ml e   3 33 378 300296

World cosmetics corporation
75111 Paris, France

SPECIAL SIZE   £7·95 RRP

Con   40%

Lab   37%

Lib   16%

Others 7%

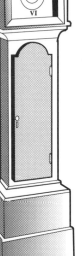

(a) Make a list of the various ways in which numbers are used in the picture.

(b) What different ways of representing numbers are used in the picture? What other ways do you know?

(c) What are the main differences between Roman numerals and modern ways of representing numbers? Are there any differences between the way numbers are represented in, for example, France and England?

(d) In the constituency represented on the pie chart, the Conservatives received 40% of the vote. What other ways are there of expressing this degree of support?

2.2 Place value

The number system which we use today is called the Hindu–Arabic system and depends upon the very simple but clever idea that the value represented by a particular digit is determined by the position of that digit in the number. For example, the digit 5 in 5 635 145 means something very different in each of the three places that it occurs.

The basic idea has been extended by the use of a decimal point. As the following story shows, great care must be taken with decimal points!

Pigs perish for a misplaced point

By Miles Barter

Birmingham City Council was this week ordered to pay massive compensation after some 250 tons of un-wanted lard were ordered for its 480 school kitchens.

A misplaced decimal point on the order form meant the city faced its own grease mountain, because only 28 tons of the cooking fat was really needed.

The firm contracted to supply the goods imported tanker-loads of pig-fat from the Continent to meet the demand. Some of the lard was intended for other ca-tering establishments but the vast bulk was intended for the schools.

A seven-year legal battle has ended with an out-of-court settlement involving a pay-out of £123,000 plus legal costs by the city.

Times Educational Supplement © Times Newspapers Ltd. 1992
24 January 1992

By trying the following problem you can see for yourself how the decimal point determines the size of a number.

A checker is paid £2·15 per thousand components.

(a) How much is this per component?

(b) How much is paid for checking ten thousand components?

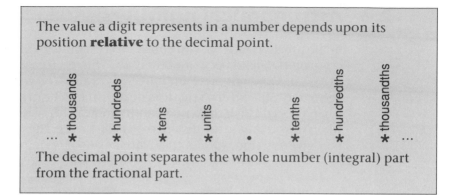

The value a digit represents in a number depends upon its position **relative** to the decimal point.

... * thousands * hundreds * tens * units . * tenths * hundredths * thousandths * ...

The decimal point separates the whole number (integral) part from the fractional part.

(a) What number is represented by the 7 in:

(i) 4·17;   (ii) 73 681·9?

(b) In the number 72·37, how many times larger is the number represented by the first 7 than that represented by the second 7?

EXERCISE 1

1 On a sheet of graph paper, using a scale of 1 cm for each unit, show the numbers 7, 0·7 and 0·07.

2 Write in figures the numbers:

(a) three thousand and seven;

(b) two hundred and nine thousand and forty-seven.

3 Put the number 358·917 on your calculator and multiply it by 10. Describe, as simply as you can, how multiplying by 10 changes the number.

4 Put a number on your calculator and describe how the number changes when you:

(a) multiply it by 100;   (b) divide it by 10;   (c) multiply it by 1000.

5 Try to do the following questions in your head, checking by calculator only if you have doubts about your answer. Write down the values of:

(a) 78×100 (b) $78 \div 100$ (c) $0·078 \times 1000$ (d) $3·6 \div 1000$

(e) $18 \times 0·0001$ (f) $1·8 \times 0·001$ (g) $1·8 \times 0·002$

6 A stack of 100 sheets of paper has a thickness of 0·8 cm. What is the thickness of each sheet?

2.3 Astronomical numbers

In the previous section, you considered examples where a checker was paid £0·002 15 per component and where a legal settlement was £123 000. Although these amounts may seem to be very small and very large respectively, scientists deal with much smaller numbers when they consider the size of atoms and vastly greater numbers when they estimate the distances between stars. The pictures below may give you some idea of the relative sizes of various objects.

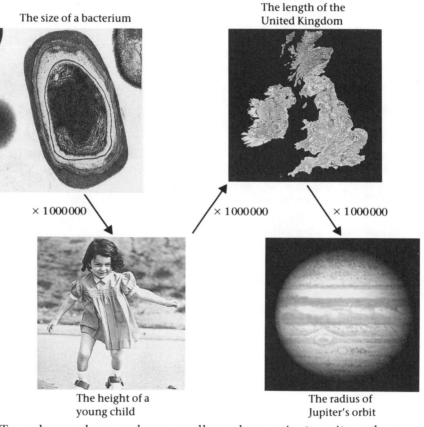

The size of a bacterium

The length of the
United Kingdom

× 1 000 000   × 1 000 000   × 1 000 000

The height of a
young child

The radius of
Jupiter's orbit

To make very large and very small numbers easier to write and say, scientists use a notation called **standard index form**.

The height of a young child is approximately 1 m. The length of the UK is roughly 1 000 000 m and the radius of Jupiter's orbit is (very roughly) 1 000 000 000 000 m. The standard forms for these distances are 10^6 m and 10^{12} m respectively. The size of a bacterium is approximately $\frac{1}{1\,000\,000}$ m and this is written as 10^{-6} m.

$$1\,000\,000 = 10^6 \quad \tfrac{1}{1\,000\,000} = 10^{-6}$$

Some further small and large numbers are as follows:

(a) the diameter of a hair is $\frac{1}{10\,000}$ m;

(b) the diameter of the Sun is 1 million km (1 thousand million metres);

(c) the diameter of an atom is $\frac{1}{10\,000\,000\,000}$ m;

(d) the distance between galaxies is 100 million million million km.

Express each of the numbers above in standard index form.

Astronomically small and large numbers are not generally equal to powers of ten. For example, the mean distance between the Sun and Earth is:

149 597 870 000 metres

This can be put into standard form as shown.

1 4 9 5 9 7 8 7 0 0 0 0 = $1 \cdot 495\,9787 \times 10^{11}$ metres

11 10 9 8 7 6 5 4 3 2 1

Note that multiplying 1·495 9787 by 10, eleven times, gives 149 597 870 000. Calculators can only store and display a certain number of digits, so they also tend to use standard form for very large and very small numbers.

What does your calculator give as the answer to:

$111\,111^2$?

EXAMPLE 1

Express the following numbers in standard form.

(a) 34 580   (b) 0·0006

SOLUTION

(a) 3 4 5 8 0 = $3 \cdot 458 \times 10^4$

(b) 0·0 0 0 6 = 6×10^{-4}

Note that 3·458 must be **multiplied** by 10 four times to give 34 580, whereas 6 must be **divided** by 10 four times to give 0·0006.

21

> Any number can be expressed in the standard form as:
>
> $$a \times 10^n$$
>
> where a is a number between 1 and 10.
>
> Thus 2×10^4 means 2 multiplied by 10 four times, i.e. 20000, whereas 2×10^{-4} means 2 divided by 10 four times, i.e. 0·0002.

EXAMPLE 2

Write down the following numbers in standard form.

(a) 10   (b) 736 billion   (c) $\frac{1}{2}$ (d) 0·00036

SOLUTION

(a) 1×10^1 (b) $736000000000 = 7·36 \times 10^{11}$

(c) $0·5 = 5 \times 10^{-1}$ (d) $3·6 \times 10^{-4}$

 TASKSHEET 1 — Using standard form (page 32)

EXAMPLE 3

If $x = 3·7 \times 10^5$ and y is $8·4 \times 10^{-6}$, find in standard form:

(a) xy (b) $\dfrac{x}{y}$

SOLUTION

(a) Key into your calculator the instructions equivalent to:

$$3·7 \boxed{EE} 5 \times 8·4 \boxed{EE} \,{}^-6$$

You should obtain 3·108.

(b) The instructions equivalent to:

$$3·7 \boxed{EE} 5 \div 8·4 \boxed{EE} \,{}^-6$$

should give an answer of approximately:

$$4·404761905 \times 10^{10}$$

EXERCISE 2

1 Which of these numbers are in standard form?

(a) 2×10^2 (b) $2{\cdot}0 \times 10^{-3}$ (c) $0{\cdot}20 \times 10^{-2}$ (d) $3{\cdot}157 \times 10^{25}$

2 A hectare is 11 960 square yards. Express this number in standard form.

3 An Italian sports car is offered for export at £83 720 and the exchange rate is 2160 lire to the pound. Express these numbers in standard form and find the price in lire of the car.

4 The diameter of the largest atom (caesium) is 0·000 000 5 mm. Write this number in standard form.

5 If $x = 2{\cdot}5 \times 10^3$ and $y = 4{\cdot}4 \times 10^{-4}$, find in standard form:

(a) xy (b) $\dfrac{x}{y}$ (c) x^2 (d) $\dfrac{1}{x} + y$

6 If $x = 2{\cdot}4 \times 10^{-5}$ and $y = 6{\cdot}5 \times 10^{-4}$, express the following numbers in standard form.

(a) xy (b) $\dfrac{x}{y}$ (c) $x + y$

7 By taking samples in a hothouse, a biologist estimates that the average mass of a grain of pollen is $2{\cdot}3 \times 10^{-5}$ g. She also estimates that, on average, each litre of air contains 340 such grains. If the volume of the hothouse is $1{\cdot}03 \times 10^5$ litres, estimate the mass of pollen in its atmosphere.

8E (a) Express in standard form the number of seconds in a year. (Assume there are 365 days in a year.)

(b) The mean distance between the Sun and Earth is called an **astronomical unit** and is 150 000 000 km. Express this number of kilometres in standard form.

(c) The gaseous ring of the Ring Nebula in the constellation Lyra has a radius of 2×10^4 astronomical units and its rate of expansion is approximately 19 km s^{-1}. Assuming this rate has remained constant, estimate how long ago the expansion started.

2.4 Equivalence

In the opening discussion point of this chapter, you may have noted that 40% meant $\frac{40}{100}$ or 40 out of 100. 40 out of 100 could be written as 4 out of 10 or as 2 out of 5.

> Write down several other equivalent expressions for 40 out of 100.

Equivalent fractions correspond to equivalent expressions:

$$\frac{40}{100} = \frac{4}{10} = \frac{2}{5}$$

The simplest form is $\frac{2}{5}$ because no number will divide into both 2 and 5.

In general:

> If the top and bottom of a fraction are multiplied or divided by the same non-zero number, then the value of the fraction is unchanged.
>
> A percentage is a fraction with denominator 100, for example:
>
> $$40\% = \frac{40}{100}$$

The idea of equivalent fractions can be used to express percentages as fractions in simplest form.

E X A M P L E   4

Express 35% as a fraction in its simplest possible form.

S O L U T I O N

$$35\% = \frac{35}{100} = \frac{7}{20}$$

There is an equivalence between fractions, decimal numbers and percentages.

E X A M P L E   5

Express 0·375 as:

(a) a fraction,   (b) a percentage.

S O L U T I O N

(a) $0 \cdot 375 = \dfrac{375}{1000} = \dfrac{5 \times 75}{5 \times 200} = \dfrac{75}{200} = \dfrac{3}{8}$

(b) $0 \cdot 375 = \dfrac{37 \cdot 5}{100} = 37 \cdot 5\%$

> To convert a fraction to a percentage, you multiply by 100.

E X E R C I S E   3

1 Express the following fractions as percentages.

(a) $\frac{1}{4}$ (b) $\frac{3}{4}$ (c) $\frac{1}{5}$ (d) $\frac{4}{5}$

2 There are about one billion Chinese in a total world population of about six billion. Express the part of the world's population which is Chinese as:

(a) a fraction,   (b) a percentage,   (c) a decimal.

3 Copy and complete this table.

Fraction	$\frac{3}{5}$		$\frac{1}{50}$			$\frac{6}{25}$
Decimal		$0 \cdot 5$			$0 \cdot 36$	
Percentage	60			12		

Percentages can be greater than 100%. For example, if the total return on a £2000 investment is £5000 then the profit is £3000 and the percentage profit is:

$\frac{3000}{2000} \times 100 = 150\%$

4 Find the percentage profit (or loss) when the return on a £2000 investment is:

(a) £3000;   (b) £1000;   (c) £6000.

2.5 Combining fractions

Fractions can be added, subtracted, multiplied and divided easily using a calculator. However, it can be convenient to know how to do some simple calculations without a calculator.

For the trainers, most people would be confident that they could quickly halve £49 and then decide whether they could afford £24·50. For the computers, the knowledge that value added tax at 17·5% increases the price by approximately $\frac{1}{6}$ would be sufficient to enable you to make a sensible comparison of the prices.

It is also easy to add or subtract fractions without a calculator, providing the fractions have the same bottom number (the **denominator**). For example, if you run a small business and distribute $\frac{1}{5}$ of the profits to each of three partners, then you are giving up $\frac{1}{5} + \frac{1}{5} + \frac{1}{5} = \frac{3}{5}$ of the profits and are therefore keeping $\frac{5}{5} - \frac{3}{5} = \frac{2}{5}$ of the profits.

In general, it is necessary to use the idea of equivalent fractions to make any fractions you wish to add or subtract have the same denominator.

EXAMPLE 6

Stephen receives some money in his grandmother's will. One-third of the money is spent on a car and half is used to repay a loan taken out when he was at college. What fraction of the money is left?

SOLUTION

The denominators are 3 and 2. Since these are both factors of 6, both fractions can be replaced by an equivalent number of sixths.

Fraction used: $\frac{1}{3} + \frac{1}{2} = \frac{2}{6} + \frac{3}{6} = \frac{5}{6}$

Fraction left: $\frac{6}{6} - \frac{5}{6} = \frac{1}{6}$

> To add or subtract fractions, first convert the fractions into equivalent fractions with the same denominator.

The way fractions can be multiplied and divided can be thought of as simple common sense. Suppose Mr and Mrs Fortune are members of a pools syndicate and each receives $\frac{1}{4}$ of the total winnings. This gives them $2 \times \frac{1}{4} = \frac{2}{4}$ or $\frac{1}{2}$. If this is then divided amongst their three children, each child receives $\frac{1}{3} \times \frac{1}{2} = \frac{1}{6}$ of the total.

In this example, the original $\frac{1}{4}$ is multiplied by 2 and then divided by 3. This calculation can be expressed in one step as:

$$\frac{2}{3} \times \frac{1}{4} = \frac{2 \times 1}{3 \times 4} = \frac{2}{12} = \frac{1}{6}$$

In general:

> $$\frac{a}{b} \times \frac{c}{d} = \frac{a \times c}{b \times d}$$
>
> Multiply the top numbers to find the top of the fraction and multiply the bottom numbers to find the denominator.

In the previous example you may have noticed that dividing by 3 is the same as multiplying by $\frac{1}{3}$. In general:

> Dividing by the fraction $\frac{c}{d}$ is the same as multiplying by $\frac{d}{c}$.
>
> $$\frac{a}{b} \div \frac{c}{d} = \frac{a}{b} \times \frac{d}{c} = \frac{a \times d}{b \times c}$$

TASKSHEET 2 — Combining fractions (page 34)

EXAMPLE 7

A number of thin washers are used to raise a hinged gate by $1\frac{1}{4}$ inches.

(a) If each washer has a thickness of $\frac{5}{64}$ inch, how many washers are used?

(b) If only half of the washers are used, by how much would the gate be raised?

SOLUTION

(a) First, replace $1\frac{1}{4}$ by $\frac{5}{4}$, then the number of washers is:

$$\frac{5}{4} \div \frac{5}{64} = \frac{5}{4} \times \frac{64}{5} = \frac{5 \times 64}{4 \times 5} = 16$$

(b) $\frac{1}{2} \times \frac{5}{4} = \frac{5}{8}$ inch

EXERCISE 4

1 Simplify:

(a) $\frac{2}{3} + \frac{5}{6}$ (b) $\frac{2}{3} - \frac{1}{2}$ (c) $1\frac{1}{2} \times \frac{2}{3}$

(d) $\frac{1}{6} \div \frac{2}{9}$ (e) $2\frac{1}{2} \div 1\frac{1}{2}$ (f) $(\frac{1}{2} + \frac{1}{3}) \times \frac{2}{3}$

2 My cat spends $\frac{2}{3}$ of each day resting and $\frac{1}{4}$ of each day hunting. What fraction of each day is left for other activities?

3 One-sixth of the students in one class went to a particular concert and two-thirds of these students obtained discounted tickets. What fraction of the whole class received cheap tickets?

4 In a local election, $\frac{3}{5}$ of the electorate voted. The Green Party received $\frac{1}{4}$ of the votes cast.

(a) What percentage of the electorate voted?

(b) What percentage of the electorate voted for the Green Party?

(c) What percentage of the electorate did **not** vote for the Green Party?

5 A stack of washers, each of thickness $\frac{3}{16}$ inch, is $1\frac{1}{2}$ inches high. How many washers are there?

2.6 **Prime numbers**

When expressing 35% as a fraction, you were able to simplify $\frac{35}{100}$ by dividing both the top and bottom of the fraction by 5. Then $\frac{35}{100} = \frac{7}{20}$. The top and bottom of the new fraction have no common factor and so $\frac{7}{20}$ is the simplest possible equivalent fraction for 35%.

Every number can be expressed as a product of factors which are prime. For example, the following **factor tree** shows 24 being split up.

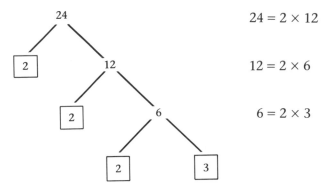

$$24 = 2 \times 12$$

$$12 = 2 \times 6$$

$$6 = 2 \times 3$$

You stop splitting when you reach prime numbers. The numbers 2, 2, 2 and 3 are prime and so cannot be factorised any further. Then $2 \times 2 \times 2 \times 3$ is one way of expressing 24 as a product of prime factors.

> (a) Work out two or three other factor trees for the number 24.
>
> (b) What do you notice about the resulting ways of expressing 24 as a product of prime factors?

E X A M P L E 8

(a) Express 36 and 150 as products of prime factors.

(b) Hence simplify the fraction $\frac{36}{150}$.

S O L U T I O N

(a) $36 = 2 \times 18 = 2 \times 2 \times 9 = 2 \times 2 \times 3 \times 3$
     $150 = 2 \times 75 = 2 \times 3 \times 25 = 2 \times 3 \times 5 \times 5$

(b) $\dfrac{36}{150} = \dfrac{\cancel{2} \times 2 \times \cancel{3} \times 3}{\cancel{2} \times \cancel{3} \times 5 \times 5} = \dfrac{6}{25}$

> A simple way of seeing if two numbers have a common factor is to express each of them as a product of prime numbers.

E X E R C I S E   5

1 (a) Express 44 and 363 as products of prime factors.

(b) Hence simplify the fraction $\frac{44}{363}$.

2 Simplify the fractions:

(a) $\frac{24}{1600}$ (b) $\frac{34}{200}$ (c) $\frac{69}{111}$ (d) $\frac{45}{125}$ (e) $\frac{96}{312}$

3 (a) How is each number in the following sequence obtained from the previous number? Write down the next two numbers.

$$3,\quad 7,\quad 15,\quad 31,\quad 63,\quad \ldots$$

(b) Those numbers in this sequence which are prime are called **Mersenne** primes. Write down the first four Mersenne primes.

(c) Mersenne primes arose from the study of perfect numbers: numbers which are equal to the sum of their factors. The only known perfect numbers are formed from Mersenne primes as follows:

$$\text{Mersenne prime} \times \frac{\text{one more than the prime}}{2}$$

For example, $3 \times \dfrac{3+1}{2} = 6$. You can easily check that 6 is perfect because its factors (excluding itself) are 1, 2 and 3, where $1 + 2 + 3 = 6$.

Find the next three perfect numbers and show the smallest of them is perfect.

4 It takes a very long time to split large numbers into their prime factors, even with a sophisticated computer to help you. This fact is used when prime numbers are applied to cryptography, the design and study of codes. It is difficult to factorise even relatively small numbers without a computer. Try the following examples – in each case the number is a product of just two primes. Use a computer or calculator to help in your search. (A table of prime numbers would also be a great help.)

(a) 14279   (b) 12091

After working through this chapter you should:

1 appreciate that there are different but equivalent ways of representing a number;

2 understand the importance of place value in the use of decimal notation;

3 be able to use standard index form to represent both very large numbers and very small numbers;

4 be able to convert between fractions, decimals, and percentages;

5 know how to add and subtract fractions using the idea of equivalence;

6 know how to multiply and divide fractions using the rules:

- $$\frac{a}{b} \times \frac{c}{d} = \frac{a \times c}{b \times d}$$

- $$\frac{a}{b} \div \frac{c}{d} = \frac{a \times d}{b \times c}$$

7 be able to express whole numbers as products of prime factors.

Using standard form

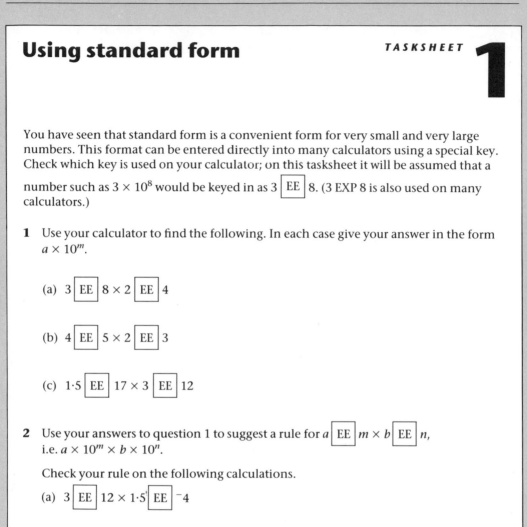

You have seen that standard form is a convenient form for very small and very large numbers. This format can be entered directly into many calculators using a special key. Check which key is used on your calculator; on this tasksheet it will be assumed that a

number such as 3×10^8 would be keyed in as 3 EE 8. (3 EXP 8 is also used on many calculators.)

1 Use your calculator to find the following. In each case give your answer in the form $a \times 10^m$.

(a) 3 EE 8 × 2 EE 4

(b) 4 EE 5 × 2 EE 3

(c) 1·5 EE 17 × 3 EE 12

2 Use your answers to question 1 to suggest a rule for a EE m × b EE n, i.e. $a \times 10^m \times b \times 10^n$.

Check your rule on the following calculations.

(a) 3 EE 12 × 1·5 EE ⁻4

(b) 6 EE 17 × 8 EE 34

3 Use your calculator to find:

(a) 8 EE 37 ÷ 4 EE 25

(b) 6 EE 41 ÷ 3 EE 21

(c) 8·4 EE 50 ÷ 2·1 EE 30

4 Suggest a rule for $a \boxed{EE} m \div b \boxed{EE} n$. Check your rule on the following calculations.

(a) $6 \boxed{EE} 12 \div 3 \boxed{EE} {}^{-}7$

(b) $1 \boxed{EE} 19 \div 2 \boxed{EE} 5$

Even if you do not key a number in using standard form, your calculator display will switch into this format if the numbers become sufficiently large or small. The following question should demonstrate this effect.

5 The speed of light is $300\,000\,000\,\text{m}\,\text{s}^{-1}$. Multiply this number successively by 60, 60, 24 and 365 to obtain the distance travelled by light in a minute, an hour, a day and a year, respectively. Your final answer is the number of metres in the distance known as a **light year**.

Combining fractions

Many rulers show both metric and imperial measurements. The inches are typically divided into halves, quarters, eighths and sixteenths.

Using a ruler like this, it is easy to appreciate why you should make fractions have the same denominator to add or subtract them.

$$\tfrac{1}{4} + \tfrac{3}{16} = \tfrac{4}{16} + \tfrac{3}{16} = \tfrac{7}{16}$$

$$1 - \tfrac{3}{16} = \tfrac{16}{16} - \tfrac{3}{16} = \tfrac{13}{16}$$

1 Use the picture of a ruler to find:

   (a) $2\tfrac{1}{2} + \tfrac{3}{16}$ (b) $3\tfrac{1}{2} - \tfrac{5}{8}$ (c) $1\tfrac{1}{4} + 2\tfrac{3}{8}$

   (d) $5\tfrac{3}{16} - 3\tfrac{1}{2}$ (e) $3\tfrac{1}{2} + 1\tfrac{7}{16}$ (f) $2\tfrac{1}{2} - 1\tfrac{9}{16}$

2 Find the perimeter of the triangle ABC.

3

Find the numbers x and y.

Multiplication of fractions can be illustrated using areas. The square below is called a **unit square** because each side is of length 1 unit. It has been divided into $4 \times 5 = 20$ equal parts.

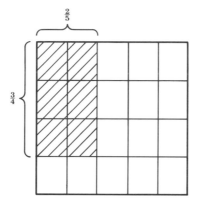

The shaded area is formed by 6 out of the 20 rectangles.

$$\frac{3}{4} \times \frac{2}{5} = \frac{3 \times 2}{4 \times 5} = \frac{6}{20} \quad \text{or} \quad \frac{3}{10}$$

4 Divide a unit square appropriately to show:

(a) $\frac{3}{5} \times \frac{3}{4}$

(b) $\frac{1}{3} \times \frac{5}{8}$

(c) $\frac{2}{7} \times \frac{3}{5}$

A unit square can also be used with fractions greater than 1.

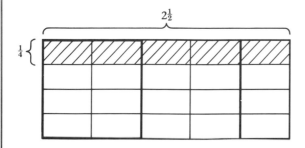

Each shaded rectangle is $\frac{1}{8}$ of the area of the unit square.

$$\frac{1}{4} \times 2\frac{1}{2} = \frac{1}{4} \times \frac{5}{2} = \frac{5}{8}$$

5 Draw pictures to illustrate:

(a) $1\frac{1}{2} \times \frac{2}{3}$

(b) $\frac{3}{4} \times 1\frac{1}{3}$

(c) $2\frac{1}{2} \times \frac{2}{5}$

3 Proportions and percentages

3.1 Scaling up or down

Here are the ingredients of a recipe for goulash which will serve six people.

---

25 ──────────── **Goulash** ────────────

900 g chuck steak   400 g onion
50 g dripping   30 g paprika
30 g flour   40 g tomato purée
400 ml stock   seasoning

> You want to make goulash for two people. What quantities do you use?

You probably decided that you had to find a third of each quantity. So, for example, the weight of onion should be:

$$\text{a third of } 400\,\text{g} = \tfrac{1}{3} \text{ of } 400\,\text{g} = \tfrac{1}{3} \times 400\,\text{g}$$
$$= 133\,\text{g} \qquad \text{(to the nearest gram)}$$

If you wanted to make a goulash for four you could calculate the weight of dripping like this.

$$\text{Two-thirds of } 50\,\text{g} = \frac{2}{3} \times 50\,\text{g}$$
$$= \frac{2 \times 50}{3}\,\text{g}$$
$$= \frac{100}{3}\,\text{g}$$

The weight of dripping is 33 g to the nearest gram.

To change from a recipe for six people to one for two or four you have to **scale down** the quantities. Increasing the quantities in a recipe involves **scaling up**.

EXAMPLE 1

A decorator mixes a trial batch of paint for a customer. The customer likes the result when one litre of yellow is mixed with three litres of white. The whole job will take 20 litres of paint. How much of each colour is needed?

SOLUTION

In the trial batch there are 4 litres of paint altogether. Since 20 litres are needed, the recipe has to be scaled up by multiplying by 5.

5 litres of yellow and 15 litres of white will be needed.

EXERCISE 1

1 Suppose you want to make goulash for yourself and three friends.

  (a) By what will you need to multiply the quantities in the recipe for six people?

  (b) Calculate the quantities that you will need, giving your answers to the nearest 5 g or 5 ml.

2 List the quantities you will need for goulash if you are having a dinner party for 15 people. Again, write all quantities to the nearest 5 g or 5 ml.

3 Find two-fifths of a mile in yards, given that a mile is 1760 yards.

4 On a packet of wallpaper paste it says that the contents are sufficient to hang 12 rolls of paper. Carmen only wants to hang 5 rolls. She weighs the packet and finds that its weight is 90 g. How much should she weigh out for her job?

5 A long-distance runner is going at a steady speed. She takes 16 minutes for 12 laps. How long will she take for 16 laps?

6 Jelly beans cost 63p for 100 g. If you ask for 50 pence-worth, what weight should you receive?

3.2 **Fair shares**

Fair shares are not always equal shares. For example, any money earned by a group of people should be shared out according to what each person put into earning the money. This is sometimes known as sharing **pro rata**.

(a) Fiona and Mary share a job in a supermarket. The weekly wage for the job is £126. Of the total of 36 hours' work, Fiona does 20. How much should Fiona receive?

(b) Clare, James and Matthew club together and bet £15 on a horse in a race. Clare puts up £3, James £5 and Matthew £7. They win £120. How should the winnings be divided up?

EXAMPLE 2

Diana, Errol and Samantha form a pools syndicate. Each week they contribute to the stake as follows:

Diana – £1·12,   Errol – 70p,   Samantha – 56p

How should they share a win of £394 468?

SOLUTION

Their contributions are in the ratio 112 : 70 : 56. The ratio numbers can all be divided by 14. This gives the ratio in its simplest form, which is 8 : 5 : 4.

Out of a total of 17 parts, Diana should have 8 parts, Errol 5 and Samantha 4.

Each part is £394 468 ÷ 17 = £23 204.

Diana should have £23 204 × 8 = £185 632.
Errol should have £23 204 × 5 = £116 020.
Samantha should have £23 204 × 4 = £92 816.

Check: 185 632 + 116 020 + 92 816 = 394 468

EXERCISE 2

1   Divide £12 000 in the ratio 7 : 23.

2   Three members of the Chandra family and two members of the Gupta family share a taxi for a journey. The taxi fare is £2·80. If the families contribute in proportion to their numbers, how much should each family contribute?

3   (a) Write the ratio 18 : 12 : 15 in its simplest form.

(b) Three partners invest £18 000, £12 000 and £15 000 respectively in a business. They agree to share the profits pro rata. The profit at the end of the year is £3255. What sums should the partners receive?

4   Tariq and Ahmed buy a present for an uncle. They agree to contribute in proportion to their weekly pocket money. Tariq has £2·40 pocket money and contributes £4·16 towards the present. Ahmed has £3 pocket money.

(a) What is the ratio of the two amounts of pocket money, in its simplest form?

(b) How much should Ahmed give towards the present?

5   Cheryl and Tracey share a job in a boutique from Monday to Friday. Cheryl works Monday to Wednesday and Tracey works the other two days. The total wage for the job is £112. How should this be shared between the two women?

3.3 **Using percentages**

Solving some problems is merely a matter of remembering that a percentage is a fraction with denominator 100. In one kind of problem you will need to calculate a percentage of a quantity. In another kind, you will need to find what percentage one quantity is of another.

E X A M P L E 3

(a) The police report that in a certain area 14% of households were burgled in 1993. There are 1450 households altogether. How many were burgled?

(b) A market researcher finds that in a sample of 240 shoppers 73 have heard of New Sudso. How does she express this as a percentage?

S O L U T I O N

(a) $14\% = \frac{14}{100} = 0 \cdot 14$
The number burgled was $0 \cdot 14 \times 1450 = 203$.

(b) As a fraction, $\frac{73}{240}$ of the sample have heard of New Sudso. As a percentage this is $\frac{73}{240} \times 100 = 30 \cdot 4\%$ (to 1 d.p.).

E X E R C I S E 3

1 Calculate:

(a) 10% of £36·20; (b) 35% of £2·80; (c) $17\frac{1}{2}$% of £135.

2 A salesman earns commission on sales at the rate of $6\frac{1}{4}$%.

(a) What is his commission for each pound of sales?

(b) In a certain month he has sales of £2660. What is his commission?

3 7·6% of the area of a county is given over to arable farming. The total area of the county is 2·43 million acres. What area is given over to arable farming?

4 Calculate what percentage the first amount is of the second.

(a) £5·04, £33·60 (b) £14·32, £763

5 A wine shop buys a certain wine at £46·20 a case of twelve bottles and sells it at £5·64 per bottle. Find the increase in price as a percentage of the cost price.

6 In a sale, the price of a pair of jeans has been marked down from £17·30 to £11·53. What percentage of the original price is the decrease?

3.4 **Percentage changes**

Increases and decreases are often described using percentages. To find the change in the amount the **original amount** must be multiplied by the percentage.

E X A M P L E   4

Rail fares are to increase by 8% in the New Year. What will be the new fare for a journey which costs £52 at present?

S O L U T I O N

8% of £52 = £52 × 0·08
　　　　　 = £4·16

The new fare will be £56·16.

> If an amount is increased or decreased by x% the actual increase or decrease is:
>
> $$\text{the original amount} \times \frac{x}{100}$$

E X A M P L E   5

What will be the cost of a holiday priced at £332 in the brochure?

LATE SEASON BREAKS
$6\frac{1}{4}$% off ALL brochure prices!

S O L U T I O N

The decrease is £332 × 0·0625 = £20·75.
The new price is £332 − £20·75 = £311·25.

EXERCISE 4

1 Increase the given amount by the given percentage.

   (a) £4·64 by 25%   (b) £730 by 37½%   (c) £52·24 by 7·3%

2 British Rail announces an increase of 8·4% on all Network fares. A commuter pays £1280 for his season ticket at present. How much will he have to pay in the future?

3 In the financial year 1991–2 the cost of living increased by 4·06%. At the beginning of the year a representative basket of commodities cost £176·24. How much did it cost at the end of the year?

4 The Bestsox hosiery firm allows its workers 32% discount off the retail price of its goods. As an employee, Mrs Green is entitled to this discount. She buys goods which would retail at £36·78. How much is she charged?

5

Angie is interested in buying a pair of jeans which had been priced at £16·60 and a blouse which had been priced at £7·80. What are the sale prices for these items?

After working through this chapter you should:

1   know how to scale quantities up and down by multiplying by fractions;

2   be able to split an amount into given proportions;

3   know how to simplify ratios;

4   be able to calculate percentage changes.

4 Managing your money

4.1 Direct taxation

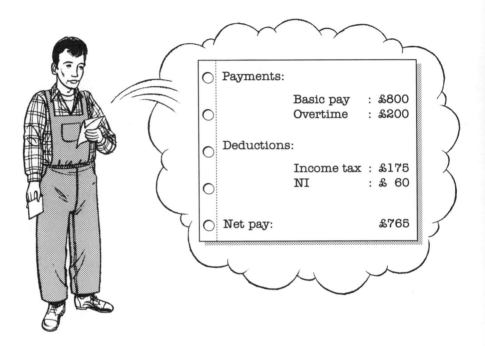

Payments:

Basic pay	: £800
Overtime	: £200

Deductions:

Income tax	: £175
NI	: £ 60

Net pay: £765

It would be wonderful if all the money you earned was yours to spend as you pleased. Unfortunately, a large slice of your income is deducted by the government before you can spend it. This form of taxation is called **direct taxation**.

There are two forms of direct taxation:

- income tax;
- National Insurance contribution.

Explain how the net pay has been calculated in the pay-slip illustrated above.

Income tax is collected by the **Inland Revenue**. When you start work, your local tax office will send you a form to fill in. This enables them to calculate your **tax-free allowance**. This is the amount you are allowed to earn before you start paying tax. Whatever you earn above your allowance is called **taxable income**.

National Insurance (NI) contributions are collected by the **Department of Social Security** (DSS). Just as with income tax, you only pay National Insurance contributions if you earn more than the **lower earnings limit**. (Paying National Insurance entitles you to benefits such as unemployment benefit, maternity allowance and retirement pension.)

All the money collected goes to the **Treasury**, where the government uses it to pay for services such as education, health, defence and for benefits such as those mentioned above.

TASKSHEET 1 – Calculating deductions (page 52)

(a) Look at the situations vacant section in a newspaper. Choose a job which you think might suit you, where the advertisement gives clear details of the pay you can expect. If necessary, calculate what the monthly or weekly pay would be.

(b) Find out what the current rates of tax are. Assume your tax allowance is the basic personal allowance. Calculate how much income tax you would have to pay each month or week.

(c) Find out what the current rates of National Insurance contributions are. Calculate how much your NI contributions would be each month or week.

(d) Calculate what your net pay would be.

(e) What percentage of your pay would be deducted?

(f) Discuss your findings with members of your class who have looked at other jobs.

EXAMPLE 1

A delivery van driver earns £400 per week. She has a tax allowance of £4200 for the year. The current rate of tax is 24%. Calculate how much income tax she would pay each week.

SOLUTION

Her weekly tax allowance is £4200 ÷ 52 = £80·77.

Her taxable income is £400 − £80·77 = £319·23.

Her income tax is 24% of £319·23 = 0·24 × 319·23
                                                  = £76·62

> A probation services assistant earns £14 640 per year. His annual tax allowance is £5740. The basic rate of tax is 27%. Calculate how much tax he pays each year if all his tax is paid at the basic rate.

EXAMPLE 2

An assistant in a florist's shop is paid £4·45 an hour for a 36-hour week. NI contributions are 2% of the first £70 earned and 9% of earnings above this lower limit. Calculate her NI contributions.

SOLUTION

Her weekly income is £4·45 × 36 = £160·20.

Her NI contributions = 2% of £70 plus 9% of £(160·20 − 70)
                                   = (0·02 × 70) + (0·09 × 90·2)
                                   = £9·52

> Suppose NI contributions are 2% of the first £234 earned each month and 9% of all remaining earnings up to an upper earnings limit of £1755. (You pay no contributions on anything you earn above the upper limit.) Calculate the maximum NI contribution you need pay.

4.2 Indirect taxation

£52·72 +VAT

£60·99 including VAT

The government also raises money by what is called **indirect taxation**. The most significant form of indirect taxation is **value added tax** or **VAT**.

When you pay for goods or services, VAT is added to the bill. The amount of VAT you pay is a percentage of the value of what you buy.

- Services are things that other people do for you. When you pay for such things as repairs to your hi-fi, or you pay someone to make a jacket for you, you pay for a service.

- Goods are things you buy such as CDs, pens, clothes, etc.

EXAMPLE 3

If the VAT rate is 20%, calculate the actual cost of a pair of trainers which are advertised as being £45 plus VAT.

SOLUTION

20% of 45 = 0·2 × 45
          = 9

The trainers cost £45 + £9 = £54.

> Which of the pairs of trainers illustrated above is cheaper if VAT is levied at 20%?

Indirect taxation differs from direct taxation in that you can choose not to pay it by not spending your money. In reality, VAT is charged on so many items that everyone pays some.

> You do not pay VAT on some goods. Make a list of goods which you think are exempt from VAT.

If you are in business and buy materials to make goods to sell to other people, then you pay VAT on the materials. When you sell the goods you have made to other people then they also pay VAT. However, this means that VAT is being paid twice on the same materials. This is unfair and so you can claim back the VAT you originally paid once you have passed it on to the customer. It is the customer who ends up paying all the VAT.

E X A M P L E   4

VAT was charged at a rate of $17\frac{1}{2}$% in 1992. Use this value in the following calculations.

(a) You buy paint costing £50 before VAT. How much VAT do you pay?

(b) You paint a customer's house and charge him £400 plus VAT for the job, including all materials. How much VAT does the customer pay?

(c) You claim back the VAT you paid for the paint. How much tax does the government end up with?

S O L U T I O N

(a) $£(0{\cdot}175 \times 50) = £8{\cdot}75$

(b) $£(0{\cdot}175 \times 400) = £70$

(c) You paid £8·75 but then claimed it back. The government only gets the £70 paid by the customer.

> Find out what the present rate of VAT is and use this to calculate the cost inclusive of VAT of an item whose cost, excluding VAT, is:
>
> (a) £3·67   (b) £579·60   (c) £36 900   (d) £0·62
>
> (e) 15p

4.3 Interest rates

Interest rate shock!

Higher interest rates means dearer mortgages, but savers benefit.

High Interest Rates Fuel Recession

The economy was in a state of panic last night due to the further rise in interest rates. This will prolong the recession until mid-summer.

German interest rates cut

The German government halted fears of more interest rate rises in Britain by lowering its base rate by 2%.

Many of its European neighbours will feel at ease this week, as their cries for

Borrowing money costs money. If you want to borrow £2000 to buy a second-hand car, then you will find that banks and other financial institutions may lend you the money, but will expect you to pay back the £2000 **plus interest**.

It also works the other way around. Financial institutions want to borrow money from you so that they in turn can lend it to other people. When you open an account with a building society, you are in effect lending the society your money. The building society pays you interest on this loan.

For example, suppose you open an account with Dolan's Bank and you invest £2000 at an annual interest rate of 8%. After one year, the bank gives you 8% of £2000 = £160 interest as payment for your lending them the money. However, during the year the bank may have lent the £2000 to someone else at 15% interest.

(a) What is 15% of £2000?

(b) What profit has the bank made on your money during the year?

TASKSHEET 2 – Calculating interest (page 54)

EXERCISE 1

1 Rosemary has a monthly salary of £2100. She has a tax allowance of £3295 and pays tax at a rate of 25%. How much income tax does she pay each month?

2 The repair bill for my car shows the costs of parts to be £89·50 and the cost of labour to be £117. VAT is then added at 17·5%. How much is the total bill?

3 Complete the following telephone bill, given that VAT is charged at 17·5% on both equipment and call charges.

```
                                            Telephone account


  CHARGES FOR TELEPHONE SERVICE ON GREENPARK 22310

  CURRENT CHARGES
       Service/equipment                      5.53
       VAT
       Service/equipment total

       Call charges                          15.60
       VAT - call charges
       Total call charges

       TOTAL AMOUNT DUE                    _____
```

4E (a) Given that the VAT rate is 17·5%, explain why an item costing £100 before VAT would cost the customer £117·50.

(b) Most prices in shops already include VAT. How much VAT has been included in the following shop prices?

(i) £117·50   (ii) £176·25   (iii) £200

5 Suppose £1000 is invested for five years at 5·75% interest. After one year the investment will have earned £57·50. Assuming this interest is left in the account the interest earned in the second year will be 0·0575 × £1057·50 = £60·81 and the account will then contain £1118·31. How much will the account contain after 5 years?

6 A leaflet for the 40th issue of National Savings certificates was as shown on page 51. The interest rates increase during the lifetime of each certificate to encourage savers to hold their certificates for the full 5 years. For a £1000 certificate:

(a) explain the amounts of interest £40, £45·76, . . ., £96·83;

(b) show how the figure of £1322·52 is obtained.

(c) By considering your answer to question 5, explain the claim that the return over 5 years is 5·75%.

How do your savings grow at 5.75%?

Here are some examples of how much 40th Issue
Certificates grow in value each year.

Interest added at end of year	£100 Certificate	£1,000 Certificate	£5,000 Certificate	Percentage increase
Year 1	£4.00	£40.00	£200.00	4.0%
Year 2	£4.58	£45.76	£228.80	4.40%
Year 3	£6.24	£62.43	£312.16	5.75%
Year 4	£7.75	£77.50	£387.51	6.75%
Year 5	£9.68	£96.83	£484.15	7.90%
Maturity value	£132.25	£1,322.52	£6,612.62	5.75% pa compound

National Savings

After working through this chapter you should:

1 be familiar with the terms:

- direct taxation,

- tax allowance,

- taxable income,

- indirect taxation,

- income tax,

- National Insurance,

- value added tax;

2 be able to calculate income tax given details of the gross pay, allowances and income tax rates;

3 be able to calculate National Insurance payments given details of the gross pay and National Insurance rates;

4 be able to calculate the VAT a business must charge and/or claim back;

5 be able to calculate the costs of borrowing money and the income from lending money.

Calculating deductions

Income tax

In the budget of March 1992, the Chancellor of the Exchequer increased personal tax allowances (a single person could earn up to £3445 a year without paying tax) and introduced a new low tax band.

Whatever you earn above your tax allowance is called taxable income and following the 1992 budget everyone paid:

- a lower rate of 20% on taxable income of £1 to £2000;

- a basic rate of 25% on taxable income of £2000 to £23700;

- a higher rate of 40% on taxable income over £23700.

A manager with a taxable income of £35000 would have paid 20% of £2000 plus 25% of £21700 plus 40% of £11300.

1 (a) Explain how the quantities £21700 and £11300 are calculated.

   (b) Calculate the manager's annual income tax bill.

2 How much income tax would she pay each month?

3 How much income tax would you pay each year if your annual taxable income was:

   (a) £1700;

   (b) £5470;

   (c) £16200?

National Insurance

In 1992, a person earning more than £234 per month would make a National Insurance contribution of:

- 2% of the first £234 earned each month;

- 9% of additional income up to an upper limit of £1755 each month.

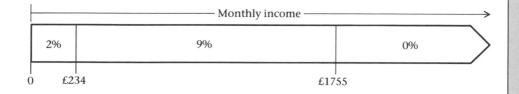

A person with a monthly salary of £2500 would pay 2% of £234 plus 9% of £(1755 − 234) = £1521. (A person earning less than £234 per month did not have to pay any contribution, but would then not have been eligible for certain benefits.)

4 Calculate the NI contribution of a person earning:

(a) £750 per month;

(b) £196 per month;

(c) £2300 per month.

Calculating interest

YOUR INTEREST RATES

Credit Interest – from 1st August 1992
(interest applied monthly)

	Gross %	Net %
On balances £10,000+	7.25%	5.43%
On balances £2,500–£9,999	6.63%	4.97%
On balances under £2,500	5.37%	4.02%

Gross
The annual rate of interest paid without deduction of basic rate income tax to eligible non-tax payers.

Net
The rates quoted are illustrative of the current gross rate less basic rate tax at the current rate of 25%.

Debit Interest – from 1st August 1992
On authorised overdrafts – 1.50% per month (19.5% APR)
On unauthorised overdrafts – 2.00% per month (26.8% APR)

Bank of Scotland (Rates correct at time of going to press but subject to variation.)

The interest on savings is classified as earnings and so most people have to pay tax on it. Usually this is deducted at source. In other words, the bank takes off an appropriate amount for tax and sends it directly to the Inland Revenue. For this reason two interest rates are quoted: one is for those people who pay tax (net interest) and the other is for people who do not (gross interest).

Use the table of interest rates given above to help you answer the following questions.

1 If you pay tax, how much interest would you earn in one year if you have:

    (a) £50 in your account;

    (b) £1000 in your account;

    (c) £5400 in your account;

    (d) £12 500 in your account.

You have an **overdraft** when you take out more money from your account than was in there in the first place. In this case the bank lends you money and you have to pay the bank interest on the loan. An authorised overdraft is one which has previously been agreed with the bank. An unauthorised overdraft is one which has not been agreed previously and the bank makes you pay extra for this.

2 (a) If you have £350 in your account and write a cheque for £500, what is your overdraft?

    (b) If the overdraft is unauthorised, how much does your overdraft cost you each month?

    (c) How much less would it have cost if the bank had previously agreed to let you have the overdraft?

5 Formulas

5.1 Algorithms

An algorithm is a sequence of simple instructions which must be followed in order to carry out a particular task. For example, suppose you wish to describe to someone how to find the area of a triangle.

You might give the following instructions.

> Measure the base, b.
> Measure the height, h.
> Multiply b by h.
> Halve the last result.

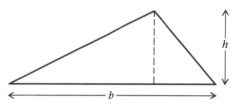

A neat way of summarising how to calculate a quantity from one or more other quantities is to give a formula. In the case above a suitable formula would be:

$A = \frac{1}{2}bh$

In many applications of mathematics, as varied as drug dosages, wallpaper coverage and mortgage repayments, you will find that those needing the information have tables of results and do not need to carry out the calculations themselves. For example, in the Highway Code, results are given for shortest stopping distances.

Shortest stopping distances (in feet)				
Speed (m.p.h.)	Thinking distance	Braking distance	Overall stopping distance	On a dry road, a good car with good brakes and tyres and an alert driver will stop in the distances shown. Remember these are shortest stopping distances. Stopping distances increase greatly with wet and slippery roads, poor brakes and tyres, and tired drivers.
20	20	20	40	
30	30	45	75	
40	40	80	120	
50	50	125	175	
60	60	180	240	
70	70	245	315	

The Highway Code

(a) Find an algorithm for converting a speed into the corresponding shortest stopping distance.

(b) What are the relative advantages and disadvantages of using a table, an algorithm or a formula in this case? Which would you use in a driving test?

5.2 **Doing things in the correct order**

There are a number of algorithms for converting temperatures between degrees Centigrade and degrees Fahrenheit. One you may not have met, but which is very easy to remember, is as follows.

To convert °F to °C

> Add 40.
> Multiply by $\frac{5}{9}$.
> Subtract 40.

Use the algorithm above to convert the following temperatures:

(a) 32°F, the freezing point of water;

(b) 212°F, the boiling point of water;

(c) ⁻40°F;

(d) *Fahrenheit 451*, the title of a Ray Bradbury novel.

The order of the instructions in an algorithm is obvious because they are already given in the correct sequence. When obtaining the equivalent formula, care must be taken to maintain this order. The formula for the temperature conversion given above is:

$$C = \tfrac{5}{9}(F + 40) - 40$$

The brackets are used to ensure that the 40 is added before the multiplication by $\frac{5}{9}$ takes place. So, if you want to use the formula:

$$C = \tfrac{5}{9}(F + 40) - 40$$

to perform a calculation on a calculator, you must be very careful either to use brackets or to calculate $F + 40$ **before** attempting the rest of the expression.

Calculators perform operations according to a strict order of priority.

1   Brackets

2   Powers and roots such as 3^5 or $5^{\frac{1}{2}} = \sqrt{5}$

3   Multiplication and division (from the left)

4   Addition and subtraction (from the left)

The significance of **from the left** is that an expression such as $8 \div 4 \div 2$ means $(8 \div 4) \div 2$ and **not** $8 \div (4 \div 2)$.

Squares and square roots usually have a separate key. These have the same priority as other powers.

For the arithmetic operations of addition and multiplication, the order in which two numbers are combined does not matter. Just as $3 + 7 = 7 + 3$ so does $3 \times 7 = 7 \times 3$. For compound measures involving division or subtraction the order is extremely important. For example, to find the density of material you might proceed as follows.

> Find the mass, $m\,$kg.
> Find the volume, $v\,$m^3.
> Divide mass by volume to find the density in kilograms per cubic metre ($\mathrm{kg\,m}^{-3}$).

(a) Write down an algorithm for determining the average speed of a car.

(b) What formula corresponds to your algorithm in part (a)?

TASKSHEET 1 — Gas bills (page 62)

EXERCISE 1

1 Use your calculator to find:

(a) $8^{\frac{1}{2}}$;

(b) $\sqrt{(51 + 62)}$;

(c) $\sqrt{5} + \sqrt{4}$;

(d) the difference between $\sqrt{5}$ and $\sqrt{2}$;

(e) the result of multiplying the sum of $\sqrt{3}$ and $\sqrt{2}$ by the difference between $\sqrt{3}$ and $\sqrt{2}$.

2 To convert pounds into francs, a bank charges £5 commission and gives an exchange rate of 9·4 francs per pound.

(a) How many francs would you receive for £300?

(b) Write down a formula for the number of francs you would receive for £P.

3 One advantage of the algorithm for temperature conversion given in this section is that the algorithm to perform the reverse conversion has the same form.

To convert °C to °F:

> Add 40.
> Multiply by $\frac{9}{5}$.
> Subtract 40.

(a) Write down a formula for this conversion, being careful to use brackets as necessary.

(b) What temperatures in °F correspond to:

  (i) absolute zero, $^-273$°C;

  (ii) $^-183$°C, the temperature at which oxygen becomes a liquid;

  (iii) $^-13$°C, the average daily temperature during a Martian summer, as measured by the Viking landing probe.

4 (a) A sequence of numbers begins as follows.

   4, 5, 7, 11, . . .

   The rule for continuing the sequence is 'each new number is obtained by doubling the last number and subtracting 3'.

   Find the next two numbers of the sequence.

(b) The same rule is used for a sequence starting with the number $^-1$. Find the first four terms of this sequence.

(c) The same rule holds for the sequence:

   $x, x, x, x, . . .$

   Find the number x.

(d) Find a formula for the new number N in terms of the last number L.

5.3 Timetables

You must take care to convert hours and minutes to a decimal number of hours when using a calculator. For example, 1 hour 30 minutes is $1 + \frac{30}{60}$ hours, that is 1·5 hours. This conversion can itself be thought of as an algorithm.

Divide the number of minutes by 60.
Add the number of hours.

> Find a formula for the average speed in m.p.h. for a journey of D miles which takes H hours M minutes.

Consider the following train timetable for journeys from Southampton to London.

Southampton and Southampton Parkway to London Waterloo
Mondays to Fridays

		1	1	1	1	1	1 A	1	1◇
		NE	NE		NE		NE	NE
		ø	ø		ø	ø	ø	ø
Southampton P	d	05 05	06 01	06 22	06 45	07 05	07 32	08 01	08 41
Southampton Parkway P ⇌	d	05 14	06 08	06 30	06 53	07 13	07 40	08 09	08 48
London Waterloo ⊖	a	06 54	07 22	07 52	08 11	08 23	08 47	09 25	10 07

		1◇	1◇	1◇	1◇		1◇	1◇ A
		NE	NE	NE	NE	and at the same minutes past each hour until	NE	
		ø	ø	ø	ø		ø	ø
Southampton P	d	09 17	09 41	10 17	10 41		15 17	15 41
Southampton Parkway P ⇌	d	09 24	09 48	10 24	10 48		15 24	—
London Waterloo ⊖	a	10 25	11 07	11 25	12 07		16 25	16 55

		1◇	1◇	1◇	1◇	1◇	1◇	1◇	1◇
		NE	NE	NE	NE	NE	NE	NE	NE
		ø	ø	ø	ø	ø	ø	ø	ø
Southampton P	d	15 44	16 17	16 41	17 17	17 41	18 17	18 41	19 17
Southampton Parkway P ⇌	d	15 52	16 24	16 48	17 24	17 48	18 24	18 48	19 24
London Waterloo ⊖	a	17 10	17 25	18 07	18 25	19 07	19 25	20 07	20 25

		1◇	1	1◇	1	1◇	1	1
		NE		NE		NE		
		ø		ø		ø		
Southampton P	d	19 41	19 50	20 41	20 50	21 46	22 05	22 50
Southampton Parkway P ⇌	d	19 48	19 59	20 48	20 59	21 54	22 14	22 59
London Waterloo ⊖	a	21 07	21 38	22 07	22 38	23 21	23 54	00 53

British Rail

For many train timetables, it is necessary to check whether the key contains important information about the services. In this case, the key is as follows:

Notes from Train columns

A	THE ROYAL WESSEX
S	Stops to set down only.
◇	Seat reservations available.
1	Also conveys First Class accommodation.
NE	Network Express service.
∅	Buffet service of hot food, sandwiches, hot and cold drinks is available for all or part of journey. Many of these trains offer a Menu service with tables near the buffet made available for customers enjoying hot meals.
⊖	Interchange for London Underground Services
⇆	Rail–Air Link
P	Car parking available – fee payable

EXERCISE 2

For the following questions, assume that the distance from Southampton to London is 77 miles.

1 Find the average speed of the 05:05 service to London.

2 (a) Which of the two Royal Wessex trains is the faster?

(b) Find the average speed of the faster train.

3 Which service is:

(a) the fastest; (b) the slowest?

In each case, find the average speed.

(c) An advertisement for this commuter line gives somewhat higher speeds for the trains. Explain why this might be justified.

4 Maria runs at 9 m.p.h. for 1 hour. She then runs for a further 30 minutes at the slower speed of 6 m.p.h.

(a) How far does she run altogether?

(b) What total time does she take?

(c) What is her average running speed for the total time?

5E   (a) A train travels at V m.p.h. for T hours. How far does it travel?

     (b) A train travels at V_1 m.p.h. for T_1 hours and at V_2 m.p.h. for T_2 hours. Find formulas for:

         (i) the total distance travelled;

        (ii) the total time taken;

      (iii) the average speed.

     (c) Use a formula to check your answer to question 4(c).

After working through this chapter you should:

1 know what is meant by an algorithm and be able to carry out a sequence of simple steps;

2 be able to convert some algorithms into formulas;

3 appreciate that the order in which arithmetic operations are performed must be carefully followed;

4 know how brackets are used to ensure that calculations in a formula are performed in the correct order;

5 be able to use simple formulas with both positive and negative numbers.

Gas bills

From 1 April 1992, gas bills throughout Europe had to be calculated using metric units. For British Gas, this meant changing from therms to kilowatt-hours even though gas meters would still register the old units. The change was explained to customers in the following leaflet.

First we need to know how much gas you have used – the volume. To do this, we take your previous meter reading away from your present reading (these are shown on the gas bill).

For example   8765 (present)
                8564 (previous)
             = 201

We then have to multiply this volume by 2.83 to convert it to cubic metres . . .

. . . 201 × 2.83 = 568.8 cubic metres.

Next we need to know how much heat was in this volume. We do this by multiplying the cubic metres (568.8 in the example above) by the 'calorific value' shown on your bill, which now has to be in metric terms. A typical calorific value is 38.1 (measured in megajoules per cubic metre). And to get kW h, we have to divide the answer by 3.6.

$$\frac{568.8 \times 38.1}{3.6} = 6019 \text{ kW h}$$

Finally, we multiply the number of kW h (units) used by the price per unit, which is shown on your gas bill. This gives the cost of the gas you have used.

Your bill is the total of the cost of the gas used and the standing charge.

Estimated Bills. If the letter 'E' is shown on your gas bill after the figure for the gas you have used, it means your bill is estimated. You may want to read the meter yourself and let us have an actual reading. See your gas bill for details. This is particularly suitable where the usual amount of gas you use has changed, for example after having new gas appliances installed.

1 (a) Using P for previous reading and N for present reading, obtain a formula for the number of kilowatt-hours. [Assume the calorific value is 38·1.]

   (b) Check your formula if $P = 8564$ and $N = 8765$. Why is your answer not quite the same as that given in the British Gas leaflet?

2 If the cost per unit is 1·5p, what would be the total cost of the units used for the meter readings:

>   8475 (present)
>   8323 (previous)

3 (a) Simplify your formula for question 1 as much as possible.

   (b) If a rough estimate is all that is required, how might your formula be made even easier?

   (c) A customer's meter readings are:

>   7530 (present)
>   7440 (previous)

   Without using a calculator, estimate the total cost of the units.

   (d) Use a calculator to check your answer to (c).

6 How accurate?

6.1 Tolerances

A student measures the length and breadth of her desk and then calculates its area. She finds the length to be 98 cm and the breadth to be 52 cm.

(a) When you measure a distance, your measurement can never be perfectly accurate. Why not?

(b) Assuming the student has measured correct to the nearest centimetre, what range of possible lengths does the measurement 98 cm represent?

(c) What does the student probably calculate the area to be?

(d) The breadth, b cm, of the desk is such that b lies between 51·5 and 52·5. Think of various different ways of expressing this range of values.

(e) What is the range of possible values for the area of the desk?

> Any measurement of length, area, weight or volume represents a range of possible values.

 TASKSHEET 1 — Tolerances (page 71)

EXAMPLE 1

A woman's height, h cm, is given as 173 cm. Write down various different ways of expressing the range of possible values for h.

SOLUTION

$h = 173$ (to the nearest whole number)
$= 173 \pm 0.5$
$= 173$ with a tolerance of 0.5

$172.5 \leqslant h < 173.5$

Note that the woman could not be 173·5 cm tall as this would have been rounded up to 174 cm. When giving a tolerance, for example 173 ± 0.5, do **not** worry about this problem of rounding.

EXERCISE 1

1 Mary fills sachets with lavender for the village fête. She puts 10 g of lavender, to the nearest gram, in each sachet.

(a) State '10 g to the nearest gram' in another way.

(b) If she makes ten sachets, what is the least weight of lavender she could use?

2 The distance of the Earth from the Sun is often given as ninety-three million miles.

(a) What is the accuracy of this measurement?

(b) Express your answer to (a) in three different ways.

3 A cube is guaranteed to have edges of 3·2 cm, correct to 1 decimal place.

(a) Express the length of an edge using a tolerance.

(b) Find the smallest and largest possible values for the volume of the cube.

(c) Express the volume of the cube using a tolerance.

4E Explain the difference between a measurement of 2·3 and one of 2·30. What do you understand by weights of 2·3 kg and 2·30 kg?

6.2 In your head

An assistant at the check-out point in a DIY store was handed ten shelf brackets, all priced at 67p. He put one over the scanner, pressed a few keys, and asked for £7·60. The customer immediately said, 'That's wrong!'

> The customer did not have a calculator. How did she know the assistant had made a mistake?

It is easy to become too dependent on machines. You possibly over-use your calculator.

E X A M P L E   1

How might you do these calculations in your head?

(a) $5 + 7 + 2 + 5 + 3$ (b) $60 \times 0{\cdot}3$

S O L U T I O N

(a) You could pair off the numbers with a sum of 10.

$$5 + 7 + 2 + 5 + 3 = 10 + 10 + 2 = 22$$

(b) Divide the first number by 10 and multiply the second number by 10.

$$60 \times 0{\cdot}3 = 6 \times 3 = 18$$

Do you remember the rule of equivalence of fractions from chapter 2?

> If the top and bottom of a fraction are multiplied or divided by the same non-zero number, then the value of the fraction is unchanged.

This rule can be useful when you want to work out divisions in your head.

EXAMPLE 2

How many 20p booklets can be purchased for £400?

SOLUTION

$$£400 \div 20p = \frac{400}{0 \cdot 2} = \frac{4000}{2} = 2000$$

(a) Where was the equivalence rule used?

(b) Give another method of answering the question.

In examples 1 and 2 you saw that:

$$60 \times 0 \cdot 3 = 18 \qquad \text{whereas} \quad 60 \times 3 = 180;$$
$$400 \div 0 \cdot 2 = 2000 \quad \text{whereas} \quad 400 \div 2 = 200.$$

These examples illustrate important results that are useful when doing calculations in your head.

Multiplying by a number greater than 1 causes an increase.
Multiplying by a number less than 1 causes a decrease.

Dividing by a number greater than 1 causes a decrease.
Dividing by a number less than 1 causes an increase.

(a) How many halves are there in 4?

(b) Evaluate $4 \div \frac{1}{2}$.

EXERCISE 2

Work these out in your head. (You can always check using your calculator.)

1 $4 + 2 + 7 + 8 + 6 + 2$ **2** $27 + 45 + 13$

3 $40 \times 0 \cdot 4$ **4** $400 \times 0 \cdot 04$

5 $60 \div 0 \cdot 3$ **6** $12 \div 0 \cdot 04$

7 Jeannie buys 3 T-shirts at £5·99 each. What is the total cost?

6.3 About right

Most people believe they have plenty of common sense but they often forget to use it when they are faced with problems in mathematics. Try to form the habit of using your common sense to make sure that:

- you understand the question;

- your answer is reasonable.

Finally, where possible:

- make a mathematical check.

> How can you check the answer to:
>
> (a) a subtraction;   (b) a division?

Where the numbers involved in a calculation are awkward you can often make a rough estimate of the answer using a mixture of common sense and approximation.

 TASKSHEET 2 – Checking a bank statement (page 72)

You can often solve problems in your head by approximating.

EXAMPLE 3

Carpet costs £14·80 a square metre. Can I cover a floor of $17\,\text{m}^2$ for £300?

SOLUTION

The price is less than £15 a square metre.
The floor area is less than $20\,\text{m}^2$.
So the cost will be less than $20 \times £15 = £300$.

When working out the cost of carpet it is not just the area of the floor that is important, but also its shape. This is because carpets are usually sold in rectangles of particular widths. However, the calculation shows that £300 will probably be enough.

Using just one or two significant figures can give you a useful rough answer to complicated calculations.

67

EXAMPLE 4

Find a rough estimate for:

$$(5 \cdot 173 \times 197 \cdot 6) \div 3 \cdot 872$$

SOLUTION

Using approximations to 1 significant figure the answer is roughly:

$$(5 \times 200) \div 4 = 1000 \div 4 = 250$$

> Use your calculator to work out the answer correct to 3
> significant figures.

EXERCISE 3

1 Without using your calculator, find the value to 1 significant figure of πr^2 if
$\pi = 3 \cdot 142$ and $r = 4 \cdot 05$.

2 My car does 32 miles to the gallon. The fuel I use costs £2·48 a gallon.
Without using your calculator, find whether £30 will be enough for a
400-mile journey.

3 Find a rough estimate for the value of:

$$(5 \cdot 93 \times 10 \cdot 4) \div 4 \cdot 09$$

4 Fiona uses her calculator to work out $4 \cdot 87 \times 418$ and gets the answer
2035·66.

Without using a calculator yourself, check this answer with a rough
estimate.

5 The 35 members of a horticultural society agree to share the cost of a bulk
purchase of bedding plants. The secretary buys 18 boxes of the plants at
£5·14 per box. He then does a calculation and announces that members will
have to pay £2·13 each.

Without using a calculator, do a rough check on the secretary's calculation.

6 A rule of thumb for converting an annual salary to an equivalent weekly
wage is double the salary and divide by 100.

Explain why this rule of thumb works.

6.4 What is the answer?

In the opening section of this chapter you saw that a rectangle of length measured to be 98 cm and of breadth measured to be 52 cm has an area which might be as small as 5021·25 cm² or as large as 5171.25 cm².

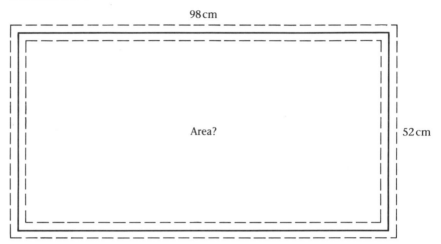

98 cm

Area?

52 cm

In this example, the measurements of length and breadth were accurate to 2 significant figures and yet the area can only be stated with confidence to 1 significant figure.

> In a calculation involving measurements, the number of significant figures in the answer should not be more than the number of significant figures in the measurements.

You may be asked to do a calculation and be given no guidance about the number of significant figures required in your answer. A sensible approach is to write out all or nearly all the figures on your calculator and follow this with a corrected answer having no more figures than appear in the numbers in the calculation. For example:

$$0·0054 \times 273 = 1·4742 = 1·5 \qquad \text{(to 2 s.f.)}$$

EXERCISE 4

In the first two questions think carefully about the accuracy of your answer.

1 A swimmer averages 48 seconds per length. How long would he take to swim 12 lengths?

2 How many seconds are there in a leap year?

3 A cricket ball is bowled at 100 m.p.h. and hits the stumps 22 yards away. For how many seconds is the ball in the air?

[There are 1760 yards in a mile.]

4 Measure the length and breadth of an A4 sheet of paper, correct to the nearest centimetre.

(a) Multiply the two numbers.

(b) Given just the two dimensions to the nearest centimetre, what would be the least and greatest possible areas of the sheet?

(c) Give a sensible value for the area in (b), using a tolerance.

After working through this chapter you should:

1 feel confident about doing simple calculations in your head;

2 be able to express approximate answers using:

- significant figures,
- decimal places,
- tolerances,
- inequalities;

3 understand the need for care in deciding the accuracy of an answer and be able to give sensible answers to calculations.

Tolerances

If the matchboxes always contain no fewer than 44 matches and no more than 52 you could say that each box holds 48 ± 4 matches.

Alternatively, you could say that the boxes hold 48 matches with a **tolerance** of 4 either way.

1 A dose of medicine is 5 ml but even with reasonable care there could be anything from $4\frac{1}{2}$ to $5\frac{1}{2}$ ml on the spoon.

Express the dose using:

  (a) a tolerance;   (b) the ± notation.

2

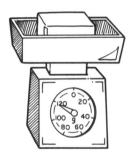

The amount of butter in the scale pan is 120 g to the nearest 5 g.

  (a) What is the least and what is the greatest possible amount of butter?

  (b) How would you express the amount using a tolerance?

In factories making small items like screws or nails, the items are examined and graded for size, using screens or gauges, between the manufacturing and packing stages. The final product then conforms to some preset standard.

3 A wood screw has a nominal length of 1·9 cm with a tolerance of 0·5 mm either way. What are its least and greatest possible lengths?

4 In a factory, nails are graded by weight. Each nail in a particular batch weighs 2 g ± 0·05 g. The nails are then packaged in plastic tubs each containing 500 g with a tolerance of 1 g either way.

  What is the greatest and what the least number of nails in a tub?
(Think carefully!)

Checking a bank statement

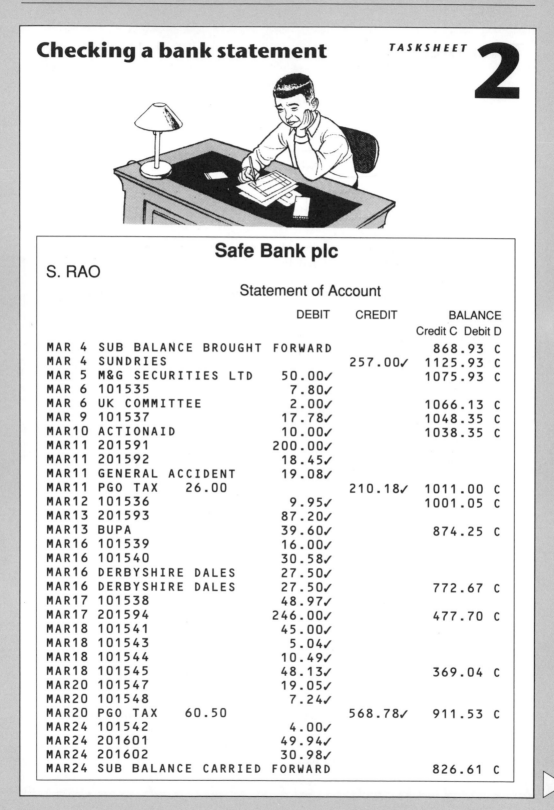

Safe Bank plc

S. RAO

Statement of Account

		DEBIT	CREDIT	BALANCE Credit C Debit D	
MAR 4	SUB BALANCE BROUGHT FORWARD			868.93	C
MAR 4	SUNDRIES		257.00✓	1125.93	C
MAR 5	M&G SECURITIES LTD	50.00✓		1075.93	C
MAR 6	101535	7.80✓			
MAR 6	UK COMMITTEE	2.00✓		1066.13	C
MAR 9	101537	17.78✓		1048.35	C
MAR10	ACTIONAID	10.00✓		1038.35	C
MAR11	201591	200.00✓			
MAR11	201592	18.45✓			
MAR11	GENERAL ACCIDENT	19.08✓			
MAR11	PGO TAX 26.00		210.18✓	1011.00	C
MAR12	101536	9.95✓		1001.05	C
MAR13	201593	87.20✓			
MAR13	BUPA	39.60✓		874.25	C
MAR16	101539	16.00✓			
MAR16	101540	30.58✓			
MAR16	DERBYSHIRE DALES	27.50✓			
MAR16	DERBYSHIRE DALES	27.50✓		772.67	C
MAR17	101538	48.97✓			
MAR17	201594	246.00✓		477.70	C
MAR18	101541	45.00✓			
MAR18	101543	5.04✓			
MAR18	101544	10.49✓			
MAR18	101545	48.13✓		369.04	C
MAR20	101547	19.05✓			
MAR20	101548	7.24✓			
MAR20	PGO TAX 60.50		568.78✓	911.53	C
MAR24	101542	4.00✓			
MAR24	201601	49.94✓			
MAR24	201602	30.98✓			
MAR24	SUB BALANCE CARRIED FORWARD			826.61	C

For any house, the commission on the first £50 000 is
2% of £50 000 = £1000.

For the first house, the commission is:

$$£1000 + 1\% \text{ of } £42\,400 = £(1000 + 0.01 \times 42\,400)$$
$$= £1424$$

For the second house the commission is:

$$£1000 + 1\% \text{ of } £55\,500 = £(1000 + 0.01 \times 55\,500)$$
$$= £1555$$

or the third house the commission is:

$$£1000 + 1\% \text{ of } £22\,800 = £(1000 + 0.01 \times 22\,800)$$
$$= £1228$$

ish's monthly income from each job would be:

job A: £540 + 2% of £3500 = £(540 + 0.02 × 3500) = £610

job B: (£120 × 52) ÷ 12 = £520

h job A she has to pay £180 for child care and so job B would be the
er option.

he effective annual pay is as follows.

oublesure: £5200 + £2300 + 5% of £100 000 = £12 500

interwarm: £7500 + 4% of £150 000   = £13 500

om the figures given, the Winterwarm job should pay £1000 per
num more than the Doublesure job.

achieve a salary of £20 000 the Winterwarm representative would
ed to earn £12 500 in commission. Since the commission rate is 4%,

$$4\% \text{ of sales over } £50\,000 = £12\,500$$
$$100\% \text{ of sales over } £50\,000 = \tfrac{100}{4} \times £12\,500$$
$$= 25 \times £12\,500 = £312\,500$$
$$\text{Total sales} = £312\,500 + £50\,000 = £362\,500$$

ployment

re the advantages and disadvantages of being self-employed?

tent the answer to this question depends on the kind of person
u might like to be your own boss or you might find it worrying.
efer to be able to organise your own working hours or you may
ne determined by someone else. You may enjoy working alone
need other people around.

fun to be able to go out for the day whenever you feel like it
not pay the bills! As a self-employed person you would need to

Mr Rao usually checks his bank statement as follows:

- He adds the amounts in the debit column to give total A.

- Then he adds the amounts in the credit column to give total B.

- Now he looks at the balance column and subtracts the last entry there from the first
  (£868·93 − £826·61 in the specimen page).

- If the statement is correct then the difference between total A and total B is the same
  as the balance difference.

1   Find the difference between total A and total B and also the balance difference for
    the specimen page.

2   Explain what you understand by the words **debit**, **credit** and **balance**. What does
    your calculation show?

When Mr Rao is pressed for time he does a rough check, rounding each amount in the
statement to the nearest £ (50p is rounded up to £1). So, in his rough check the balance
has gone down from £869 to £827.

3   Find the difference between total A and total B and also the balance difference when
    he does a rough check on the specimen page. Would you say that the rough check
    has succeeded?

4   On another page of Mr Rao's statement there are again 26 items in the debit column
    and 3 items in the credit column. In a rough check, he finds that the two differences
    (A − B and the balance difference) are nothing like the same. He does an accurate
    check and finds that the statement is correct after all.

    (a) What kind of amounts of money in the debit column could result in a bad
         failure of the rough check?

    (b) Why are such failures not common?

    (c) In a page with 26 items in the debit column and 3 items in the credit column:

         (i) describe the situation which would result in the worst failure of a rough
              check.

         (ii) How far apart would the difference in totals A and B and the balance
              difference be in this case?

Solutions

1 The world of work

1.1 Piece-rates

EXERCISE 1

1 She earns $53 \times 84\text{p} = 4452\text{p} = £44\cdot52$.

2 (a) £6·30 per hundred = £63 per thousand

   (b) For 2200 envelopes she earns $2 \times £63 + 2 \times £6\cdot30 = £138\cdot60$.

3 The number of pairs at £1·60 is $10 + 9 + 8 + 10 + 10 = 47$ giving $47 \times £1\cdot60 = £75\cdot20$.

   The number at £3·20 is $3 + 2 + 4 = 9$ giving $9 \times £3\cdot20 = £28\cdot80$.

   Ali's total wage is $£42 + £75\cdot20 + £28\cdot80 = £146$.

4 The total payments under each method are as follows.
   Method A: $£64 + 48 \times £2\cdot60 = £188\cdot80$
   Method B: $48 \times £4\cdot30 = £206\cdot40$
   Method B should be chosen.

5 The weekly quota is $1500 \times 5 = 7500$.
   Margaret earns the bonus on $10\,220 - 7500 = 2720$ boxes.
   The bonus is $272 \times 12\text{p} = £32\cdot64$.
   Her wage is $£116 + £32\cdot64 = £148\cdot64$.

1.2 Time-rates

> (a) Maria is a computer operator. She works a 36-hour week and her hourly rate is £8·24. What is her monthly salary? (Assume that there are precisely 52 weeks in a year.)
>
> (b) Andrew works a 38-hour week for which his pay is £126·92. What is his hourly rate?

(a) Her weekly pay is $36 \times £8\cdot24 = £296\cdot64$, so her annual salary is $52 \times £296\cdot64 = £15\,425\cdot28$. This is paid in twelve equal monthly amounts, each of $£15\,425\cdot28 \div 12 = £1285\cdot44$.

(b) The pay for one hour is the pay for 38 hours $\div\, 38 = £126\cdot92 \div 38$
                                          $= £3\cdot34$

Maria's time of clocking in and ou

Day	In
Monday	09:30
Tuesday	08:45
Wednesday	09:00
Thursday	09:15
Friday	08:45

At what time must she clo
complete her 36 hours?

The times worked up to the

   Mon: $6\frac{1}{2}$ h   Tue:

These times total $31\frac{1}{4}$ hou
$(36 - 31\frac{1}{4})$ hours = $4\frac{3}{4}$ ho

EXERCISE 2

1 The equivalent numbe
   giving a wage of $56 \times$

2 The equivalent num
       $38 + (14 \times 1\frac{1}{2})$
   giving a wage of 67

3 Leila works for $7\frac{3}{4}$
   Thursday she has
   hours and so cloc

4 (a) The basic h
   (b) Gopal's ov
       The overti
       The numb

1.3 Commissi

EXERCI

1 The salesr

   £85

76

1.4 Self-em

> What a

To some e
you are. Yo
You may p
need a rout
or you may

It may soun
but it would

be organised and keep careful financial records or you could have tremendous problems with the tax office! You would not be paid for holidays or sickness and you would have to arrange your own pension and insurance. On the other hand it is often said that no one becomes really rich by working for someone else.

EXERCISE 4

1 The costs are:

netting	£165·60
standard posts	£345
corner posts	£75·60
staples	£3·40
labour	£90
Total	£679·60

If the netting is charged for by the roll it would cost £180 and the total would then be £694.

2

	£
Depreciation	4800
Maintenance	1400
Fuel	2300
Total expenses	8500

3E **Profit and loss account**

	£	£
Total income		29 460
Less operating expenses		
Rent, rates	6720	
Electricity	560	
Telephone	420	
Postage	780	
Stationery and printing	680	9 160
Operating profit		20 300
Less salary		20 300
Retained profits		0

2 Using numbers

2.2 Place value

> A checker is paid £2·15 per thousand components.
>
> (a) How much is this per component?
>
> (b) How much is paid for checking ten thousand components?

(a) £0·002 15 or 0·215p

(b) £21·50

> (a) What number is represented by the 7 in:
>
>   (i) 4·17;   (ii) 73 681·9?
>
> (b) In the number 72·37, how many times larger is the number
> represented by the first 7 than that represented by the second 7?

(a) (i) Seven hundredths   (ii) Seventy thousand

(b) The first 7 is one thousand times larger than the second 7.

EXERCISE 1

1

								7
	0·7							
0·07								

2 (a) 3007   (b) 209 047

3 The decimal point moves one place to the right:

$$358·917 \times 10 = 3589·17$$

Mr Rao usually checks his bank statement as follows:

• He adds the amounts in the debit column to give total A.

• Then he adds the amounts in the credit column to give total B.

• Now he looks at the balance column and subtracts the last entry there from the first (£868·93 − £826·61 in the specimen page).

• If the statement is correct then the difference between total A and total B is the same as the balance difference.

1 Find the difference between total A and total B and also the balance difference for the specimen page.

2 Explain what you understand by the words **debit**, **credit** and **balance**. What does your calculation show?

When Mr Rao is pressed for time he does a rough check, rounding each amount in the statement to the nearest £ (50p is rounded up to £1). So, in his rough check the balance has gone down from £869 to £827.

3 Find the difference between total A and total B and also the balance difference when he does a rough check on the specimen page. Would you say that the rough check has succeeded?

4 On another page of Mr Rao's statement there are again 26 items in the debit column and 3 items in the credit column. In a rough check, he finds that the two differences (A − B and the balance difference) are nothing like the same. He does an accurate check and finds that the statement is correct after all.

   (a) What kind of amounts of money in the debit column could result in a bad failure of the rough check?

   (b) Why are such failures not common?

   (c) In a page with 26 items in the debit column and 3 items in the credit column:

     (i) describe the situation which would result in the worst failure of a rough check.

     (ii) How far apart would the difference in totals A and B and the balance difference be in this case?

Solutions

1 The world of work

1.1 Piece-rates

E X E R C I S E   1

1 She earns $53 \times 84p = 4452p = £44 \cdot 52$.

2 (a) $£6 \cdot 30$ per hundred $= £63$ per thousand

(b) For 2200 envelopes she earns $2 \times £63 + 2 \times £6 \cdot 30 = £138 \cdot 60$.

3 The number of pairs at $£1 \cdot 60$ is $10 + 9 + 8 + 10 + 10 = 47$ giving $47 \times £1 \cdot 60 = £75 \cdot 20$.

The number at $£3 \cdot 20$ is $3 + 2 + 4 = 9$ giving $9 \times £3 \cdot 20 = £28 \cdot 80$.

Ali's total wage is $£42 + £75 \cdot 20 + £28 \cdot 80 = £146$.

4 The total payments under each method are as follows.
Method A: $£64 + 48 \times £2 \cdot 60 = £188 \cdot 80$
Method B: $48 \times £4 \cdot 30 \qquad = £206 \cdot 40$
Method B should be chosen.

5 The weekly quota is $1500 \times 5 = 7500$.
Margaret earns the bonus on $10220 - 7500 = 2720$ boxes.
The bonus is $272 \times 12p = £32 \cdot 64$.
Her wage is $£116 + £32 \cdot 64 = £148 \cdot 64$.

1.2 Time-rates

(a) Maria is a computer operator. She works a 36-hour week and her hourly rate is $£8 \cdot 24$. What is her monthly salary? (Assume that there are precisely 52 weeks in a year.)

(b) Andrew works a 38-hour week for which his pay is $£126 \cdot 92$. What is his hourly rate?

(a) Her weekly pay is $36 \times £8 \cdot 24 = £296 \cdot 64$, so her annual salary is $52 \times £296 \cdot 64 = £15\,425 \cdot 28$. This is paid in twelve equal monthly amounts, each of $£15\,425 \cdot 28 \div 12 = £1285 \cdot 44$.

(b) The pay for one hour is the pay for 38 hours $\div 38 = £126 \cdot 92 \div 38$
$$= £3 \cdot 34$$

Maria's time of clocking in and out in a particular week are as follows:

Day	In	Out	In	Out
Monday	09:30	13:00	13:45	16:45
Tuesday	08:45	12:45	13:15	16:45
Wednesday	09:00	12:45	13:30	16:45
Thursday	09:15	13:00	14:00	16:30
Friday	08:45	12:45	13:15	

At what time must she clock out on Friday afternoon if she is to complete her 36 hours?

The times worked up to the final session are:

Mon: $6\frac{1}{2}$h　　Tue: $7\frac{1}{2}$h　　Wed: 7h　　Thu: $6\frac{1}{4}$h　　Fri: 4h

These times total $31\frac{1}{4}$ hours, so on Friday afternoon she must work for $(36 - 31\frac{1}{4})$ hours $= 4\frac{3}{4}$ hours. As she starts at 13:15 she will finish at 18:00.

EXERCISE 2

1　The equivalent number of hours at standard rate is $8 + (32 \times 1\frac{1}{2}) = 56$ giving a wage of $56 \times £5{\cdot}24 = £293{\cdot}44$.

2　The equivalent number of hours at standard rate is:

$$38 + (14 \times 1\frac{1}{2}) + (4 \times 2) = 67$$

giving a wage of $67 \times £4{\cdot}26 = £285{\cdot}42$.

3　Leila works for $7\frac{3}{4}$ hours per day from Monday to Thursday. By the end of Thursday she has worked $7\frac{3}{4} \times 4 = 31$ hours. On Friday she must work 5 hours and so clocks off $2\frac{3}{4}$ hours earlier than usual, at 2:45 p.m.

4　(a)　The basic hourly rate is $£157{\cdot}70 \div 38 = £4{\cdot}15$.

　　(b)　Gopal's overtime pay is $£207{\cdot}50 - £157{\cdot}70 = £49{\cdot}80$.
　　　　The overtime rate is $1\frac{1}{2} \times £4{\cdot}15 = £6{\cdot}23$ (to the nearest penny).
　　　　The number of hours of overtime is $49{\cdot}80 \div 6{\cdot}23 = 8$.

1.3　Commission

EXERCISE 3

1　The salesman's salary is:

$$£850 + 10\% \text{ of } £13\,400 = £(850 + 0{\cdot}1 \times 13\,400)$$
$$= £2190$$

2 For any house, the commission on the first £50 000 is
2% of £50 000 = £1000.

For the first house, the commission is:

$$£1000 + 1\% \text{ of } £42\,400 = £(1000 + 0{\cdot}01 \times 42\,400)$$
$$= £1424$$

For the second house the commission is:

$$£1000 + 1\% \text{ of } £55\,500 = £(1000 + 0{\cdot}01 \times 55\,500)$$
$$= £1555$$

For the third house the commission is:

$$£1000 + 1\% \text{ of } £22\,800 = £(1000 + 0{\cdot}01 \times 22\,800)$$
$$= £1228$$

3 Trish's monthly income from each job would be:

job A: £540 + 2% of £3500 = £(540 + 0·02 × 3500) = £610

job B: (£120 × 52) ÷ 12 = £520

With job A she has to pay £180 for child care and so job B would be the
better option.

4 (a) The effective annual pay is as follows.

Doublesure: £5200 + £2300 + 5% of £100 000 = £12 500

Winterwarm: £7500 + 4% of £150 000   = £13 500

From the figures given, the Winterwarm job should pay £1000 per
annum more than the Doublesure job.

(b) To achieve a salary of £20 000 the Winterwarm representative would
need to earn £12 500 in commission. Since the commission rate is 4%,

$$4\% \text{ of sales over } £50\,000 = £12\,500$$
$$100\% \text{ of sales over } £50\,000 = \tfrac{100}{4} \times £12\,500$$
$$= 25 \times £12\,500 = £312\,500$$
$$\text{Total sales} = £312\,500 + £50\,000 = £362\,500$$

1.4 Self-employment

What are the advantages and disadvantages of being self-employed?

To some extent the answer to this question depends on the kind of person
you are. You might like to be your own boss or you might find it worrying.
You may prefer to be able to organise your own working hours or you may
need a routine determined by someone else. You may enjoy working alone
or you may need other people around.

It may sound fun to be able to go out for the day whenever you feel like it
but it would not pay the bills! As a self-employed person you would need to

4   The decimal point moves:

(a) two places to the right;

(b) one place to the left;

(c) three places to the right.

5   (a) 7800   (b) 0·78   (c) 78   (d) 0·0036

(e) 0·0018   (f) 0·0018   (g) 0·0036

6   0·008 cm

2.3   Astronomical numbers

> Express each of the numbers above in standard index form.

(a) 10^{-4} m

(b) 1 million = 1 000 000 = 10^6 km
     (or 1 thousand million = 1 000 000 000 = 10^9 m)

(c) 10^{-10} m

(d) 10^{20} km or 10^{23} m

> What does your calculator give as the answer to:
> $111\,111^2$?

The author's calculator gave 1·234 565 432 E 10, meaning:

$$1\cdot234\,565\,432 \times 10^{10} = 1\,2\,3\,4\,5\,6\,5\,4\,3\,2\,0$$

The accurate answer is 12 345 654 321.

EXERCISE 2

1   (a), (b) and (d) are in standard form.

For (c), $0\cdot2 \times 10^{-2}$ is equal to 2×10^{-3} in standard form.

2 $1\cdot196 \times 10^4$ square yards

3   £$8\cdot372 \times 10^4$
     $2\cdot16 \times 10^3$ lire to the pound
     $8\cdot372 \times 2\cdot16 \times 10^7 \approx 18\cdot08 \times 10^7 = 1\cdot808 \times 10^8$ lire

4 5×10^{-7} mm

5   (a) 1·1

     (b) $5 \cdot 68 \times 10^6$

     (c) $6 \cdot 25 \times 10^6$

     (d) $\dfrac{1}{x} = 4 \times 10^{-4}$

        $\dfrac{1}{x} + y = 8 \cdot 4 \times 10^{-4}$

6   (a) $15 \cdot 6 \times 10^{-9} = 1 \cdot 56 \times 10^{-8}$

     (b) $0 \cdot 369 \times 10^{-1} = 3 \cdot 69 \times 10^{-2}$

     (c) $0 \cdot 24 \times 10^{-4} + 6 \cdot 5 \times 10^{-4} = 6 \cdot 74 \times 10^{-4}$

7    $2 \cdot 3 \times 10^{-5} \times 340 \times 1 \cdot 03 \times 10^5 = 8 \cdot 05 \times 10^2$ or $805\,\mathrm{g}$

8E   (a) $60 \times 60 \times 24 \times 365 = 31\,536\,000$

                                   $= 3 \cdot 1536 \times 10^7$

     (b) $1 \cdot 5 \times 10^8\,\mathrm{km}$

     (c) $\dfrac{2 \times 10^4 \times 1 \cdot 5 \times 10^8}{19} \approx 1 \cdot 5789 \times 10^{11}$ seconds

                        $\approx \dfrac{1 \cdot 5789 \times 10^{11}}{3 \cdot 1536 \times 10^7}$ years

                        $\approx 0 \cdot 5007 \times 10^4$ years

                        $\approx 5 \times 10^3$ years

2.4   Equivalence

> Write down several other equivalent expressions for 40 out of 100.

Just a few of the forms possible are:

      400 out of 1000
      20 out of 50
      10 out of 25
      8 out of 20
      6 out of 15

E X E R C I S E   3

1   (a) 25%   (b) 75%   (c) 20%   (d) 80%

2   (a) $\frac{1}{6}$

(b) Approximately 16·7%

(c) Approximately 0·167

3

Fraction	$\frac{3}{5}$	$\frac{1}{2}$	$\frac{1}{50}$	$\frac{3}{25}$	$\frac{9}{25}$	$\frac{6}{25}$
Decimal	0·6	0·5	0·02	0·12	0·36	0·24
Percentage	60	50	2	12	36	24

4   (a) $\frac{1000}{2000} \times 100 = 50\%$ (profit)

(b) $\frac{1000}{2000} \times 100 = 50\%$ (loss)

(c) $\frac{4000}{2000} \times 100 = 200\%$ (profit)

2.5   Combining fractions

E X E R C I S E   4

1   (a) $\frac{4}{6} + \frac{5}{6} = \frac{9}{6} = \frac{3}{2} = 1\frac{1}{2}$

(b) $\frac{4}{6} - \frac{3}{6} = \frac{1}{6}$

(c) $\frac{3}{2} \times \frac{2}{3} = 1$

(d) $\frac{1}{6} \times \frac{9}{2} = \frac{9}{12} = \frac{3}{4}$

(e) $\frac{5}{2} \div \frac{3}{2} = \frac{5}{2} \times \frac{2}{3} = \frac{5}{3} = 1\frac{2}{3}$

(f) $\frac{5}{6} \times \frac{2}{3} = \frac{10}{18} = \frac{5}{9}$

2 $\frac{2}{3} + \frac{1}{4} = \frac{8}{12} + \frac{3}{12} = \frac{11}{12}$

$\frac{12}{12} - \frac{11}{12} = \frac{1}{12}$

(This means that 16 hours are spent resting and 6 hours hunting, leaving $\frac{1}{12} \times 24 = 2$ hours for other activities.)

3 $\frac{2}{3} \times \frac{1}{6} = \frac{2 \times 1}{3 \times 6} = \frac{1}{9}$

4   (a) $\frac{3}{5} \times 100 = 60\%$

(b) $60 \times \frac{1}{4} = 15\%$

(c) $100 - 15 = 85\%$

5 $\frac{3}{2} \div \frac{3}{16} = \frac{3}{2} \times \frac{16}{3} = 8$

2.6 Prime numbers

(a) Work out two or three other factor trees for the number 24.

(b) What do you notice about the resulting ways of expressing 24 as a product of prime factors?

(a) Just two of the various possibilities are:

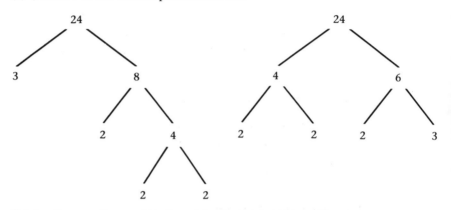

(b) In all cases, the result is the same product of primes (in some order):

$$24 = 2 \times 2 \times 2 \times 3$$

Part of the importance of prime numbers stems from the fact that each number can be expressed in a **unique** way as a product of primes.

EXERCISE 5

1   (a) $44 = 2 \times 2 \times 11$
         $363 = 3 \times 11 \times 11$

    (b) $\frac{44}{363} = \frac{4}{33}$

2   (a) $\frac{3}{200}$ (b) $\frac{17}{100}$ (c) $\frac{23}{37}$ (d) $\frac{9}{25}$ (e) $\frac{4}{13}$

3   (a) Each number is obtained by doubling the previous number and adding one. The next two numbers are 127 and 255.

    (b) 3, 7, 31, 127

    (c) The first four perfect numbers are:

         $3 \times 2 = 6$
         $7 \times 4 = 28$
         $31 \times 16 = 496$
         $127 \times 64 = 8128$

         For example, $28 = 1 + 2 + 4 + 7 + 14$

4   (a) 109×131 (b) 107×113

3 Proportions and percentages

3.1 Scaling up or down

> You want to make goulash for two people. What quantities do you use?

300 g chuck steak	133 g onion
17 g dripping	10 g paprika
10 g flour	13 g tomato purée
133 ml stock	seasoning

EXERCISE 1

1 (a) The quantities in the original recipe should be multiplied by $\frac{4}{6} = \frac{2}{3}$.

(b)
600 g chuck steak	265 g onion
35 g dripping	20 g paprika
20 g flour	25 g tomato purée
265 ml stock	seasoning

2 The quantities in the original recipe should be multiplied by $\frac{15}{6} = \frac{5}{2}$.

2250 g chuck steak	1000 g onion
125 g dripping	75 g paprika
75 g flour	100 g tomato purée
1000 ml stock	seasoning

3 704 yards

4 $\frac{5}{12} \times 90\,g = 37 \cdot 5\,g$

To be on the safe side Carmen would probably use 40 g.

5 $16 \times \frac{16}{12} = 21\frac{1}{3}$ minutes (21 minutes 20 seconds)

6 $100 \times \frac{50}{63} = 79\,g$ (to the nearest gram)

3.2 Fair shares

EXERCISE 2

1 For a ratio 7 : 23 there are $7 + 23 = 30$ parts altogether.
Each part is £12 000 ÷ 30 = £400.
The two amounts are $7 \times £400 = £2800$ and $23 \times £400 = £9200$.

Check: £2800 + £9200 = £12 000

2   They should contribute in the ratio 3 : 2.
There are 3 + 2 = 5 parts altogether. Each part is £2·80 ÷ 5 = 56p.
The Chandras pay 56p × 3 = £1·68; the Guptas pay 56p × 2 = £1·12.

Check: £1·68 + £1·12 = £2·80

3   (a) 6 : 4 : 5

(b) The profit should be shared in the ratio 6 : 4 : 5 (15 parts).
The partners should receive £1302, £868 and £1085 respectively.

Check: £1302 + £868 + £1085 = £3255

4   (a) 240 : 300 = 4 : 5 (dividing each ratio number by 60)

(b) Ahmed should give $\frac{5}{4}$ × £4·16 = £5·20.

5   The daily wage is £112 ÷ 5 = £22·40
Cheryl should have 3 × £22·40 = £67·20.
Tracey should have 2 × £22·40 = £44·80.

Check: the two shares total £112.

3.3   Using percentages

E X E R C I S E   3

1   (a) £3·62   (b) 98p   (c) £23·63 (to the nearest penny)

2   (a) 6·25p

(b) 2660 × 6·25p = £166·25

3 $\dfrac{7·6}{100}$ × 2·43 million acres ≈ 185 000 acres

4   (a) 15%   (b) 1·88%   (to 3 d.p.)

5   The wine is sold for 12 × £5·64 = £67·68
The increase in price for the case is £67·68 − £46·20 = £21·48.
As a percentage of the cost price this is $\dfrac{21·48}{46·20}$ × 100 = 46·5%   (to 1 d.p.).

6   The decrease is £5·77.
As a percentage of the original price this is $\dfrac{5·77}{17·3}$ × 100 = 33·4%   (to 1 d.p.).

3.4 Percentage changes

EXERCISE 4

1 (a) £4·64 × 1·25 = £5·80   (b) £1003·75   (c) £56·05

2 £1280 × 1·084 = £1387·52
If season ticket prices are rounded to the nearest £10, the price would be £1390.

3 £176·24 × 1·0406 = £183·40   (to the nearest penny)

4 If 32% discount is given, the workers pay 68% of the retail price.
Mrs Green is charged $\frac{68}{100}$ × £36·78 = £25·01.

5 15% of £16·60 = £16·60 × 0·15 = £2·49
The sale price for the jeans is:

£(16·60 − 2·49) = £14·11

15% of £7·80 = £7·80 × 0·15 = £1·17
The sale price for the blouse is:

£(7·80 − 1·17) = £6·63

4 Managing your money

4.1 Direct taxation

> Explain how the net pay has been calculated in the pay-slip illustrated above.

Total pay before deductions is called **gross** pay. In this case the gross pay is £800 + £200 = £1000.

The total deductions are £175 + £60 = £235.

Net pay is gross pay less all deductions, which in this case gives £1000 − £235 = £765.

> A probation services assistant earns £14 640 per year. His annual tax allowance is £5740. The basic rate of tax is 27%. Calculate how much tax he pays each year if all his tax is paid at the basic rate.

Annual taxable income   = £14 640 − £5740 = £8900

Annual tax is 27% of £8900 = 0·27 × 8900
= £2403

Suppose NI contributions are 2% of the first £234 earned each month and 9% of all remaining earnings up to an upper earnings limit of £1755. (You pay no contributions on anything you earn above the upper limit.) Calculate the maximum NI contribution you need pay.

$$
\begin{aligned}
\text{Maximum National Insurance contribution} &= \text{2\% of £234 + 9\% of £1521} \\
&= 0{\cdot}02 \times £234 + 0{\cdot}09 \times £1521 \\
&= £141{\cdot}57
\end{aligned}
$$

4.2 Indirect taxation

Which of the pairs of trainers illustrated above is cheaper if VAT is levied at 20%?

$$
\begin{aligned}
£52{\cdot}72 + \text{VAT} &= £52{\cdot}72 + \text{20\% of £52.72} \\
&= £52{\cdot}72 + 0{\cdot}2 \times £52{\cdot}72 \\
&= £63{\cdot}264 \\
&= £63{\cdot}26
\end{aligned}
$$

These trainers are more expensive than £60·99. The cheaper trainers are therefore the ones costing £60·99.

You do not pay VAT on some goods. Make a list of goods which you think are exempt from VAT.

The following are some of the goods which were exempt from VAT in 1992:

- food;
- children's clothes;
- books;
- newspapers and magazines.

Find out what the present rate of VAT is and use this to calculate the cost inclusive of VAT of an item whose cost, excluding VAT, is:

(a) £3·67   (b) £579·60   (c) £36 900   (d) £0·62   (e) 15p

If the present rate of VAT is $17\frac{1}{2}$% then the items cost:

(a) £4·31   (b) £681·03   (c) £43 357·50   (d) £0·73   (e) 18p

All amounts are rounded to the nearest penny.

4.3   Interest rates

(a) What is 15% of £2000?

(b) What profit has the bank made on your money during the year?

(a) 15% of £2000 = 0·15 × 2000
                        = £300
(b) The bank has made a profit of £(300 − 160) = £140.

E X E R C I S E   1

1   Her monthly tax allowance is £3295 ÷ 12 = £274·58.
Her taxable income each month is £(2100 − 274·58) = £1825·42.
Her income tax is 0·25 × £1825·42 = £456·36.

2   £(89·50 + 117) = £206·50
0·175 × £206·50 = £36·14
The total bill is £242·64.

3
Service/equipment	5·53
VAT	0·97
Service/equipment total	6·50
Call charges	15·60
VAT – call charges	2·73
Total call charges	18·33
Total amount due	24·83

4E (a) The VAT is 17·5% of £100 = 0·175 × £100 = £17·50.
           The cost including VAT is £(100 + 17·50) = £117·50.

(b) (i) £17·50   (from (a))

   (ii) $\dfrac{176·25}{117·50} \times £17·50 = £26·25$

   (iii) $\dfrac{200}{117·50} \times £17·50 = £29·79$

5   After year 1 the account contains £1057·50.
After year 2 the account contains £1118·31.
After year 3 the account contains £1182·61.
After year 4 the account contains £1250·61.
After year 5 the account contains £1322·52.

6   (a)   0·04 × £1000 = £40
                 0·044 × £1040 = £45·76
              0·0575 × £1085·76 = £62·43
              0·0675 × £1148·19 = £77·50
               0·079 × £1225·69 = £96·83

4   (a) $9 + \frac{1}{2} \times 6 = 12$ miles

       (b) $1\frac{1}{2}$ hours

       (c) $12 \div 1\frac{1}{2} = 8$ m.p.h.

5E   (a)   It travels VT miles.

       (b)   (i) $V_1 T_1 + V_2 T_2$

           (ii) $T_1 + T_2$

           (iii) $\dfrac{V_1 T_1 + V_2 T_2}{T_1 + T_2}$

       (c) $\dfrac{9 \times 1 + 6 \times \frac{1}{2}}{1 + \frac{1}{2}} = \dfrac{12}{1\frac{1}{2}} = 8$ m.p.h.

It is important to note that average speeds cannot be found by simply averaging the speeds. You have to take into account the **time** travelled at each speed.

6 How accurate?

6.1   Tolerances

EXERCISE 1

1   (a)   Mary puts $10\text{g} \pm \frac{1}{2}\text{g}$ in each sachet.

       (b)   The least weight is $9.5\text{g} \times 10 = 95\text{g}$.

2   (a)   The accuracy is to the nearest million miles.

       (b)   The distance is $93\,000\,000$ miles $\pm\, 500\,000$ miles.
The distance is $93\,000\,000$ miles to 2 significant figures.
The distance lies between $92\,500\,000$ miles and $93\,500\,000$ miles.

3   (a)   The length is $3.2\,\text{cm} \pm 0.05\,\text{cm}$.

       (b)   The volume could be anywhere between:

$$3.15^3 = 31.3\,\text{cm}^3 \quad \text{(to 1 d.p.)}$$

and:

$$3.25^3 = 34.3\,\text{cm}^3 \quad \text{(to 1 d.p.)}$$

       (c)   A reasonable answer using a tolerance would be $32.8\,\text{cm}^3 \pm 1.5\,\text{cm}^3$. This shows how small errors can lead to large errors after a couple of multiplications.

4E A measurement of 2·3 would be taken to be between 2·25 and 2·35, while one of 2·30 would be taken to be between 2·295 and 2·305.

A weight of 2·3 kg would be 2300 g to the nearest 50 g, while one of 2·30 kg would be 2300 g to the nearest 5 g.

6.2 In your head

> The customer did not have a calculator. How did she know the assistant had made a mistake?

The customer probably performed the easy mental calculation:

67p × 10 = £6·70.

> (a) Where was the equivalence rule used?
>
> (b) Give another method of answering the question.

(a) The equivalence rule was used in the step $\dfrac{400}{0·2} = \dfrac{4000}{2}$, where the

top and bottom of the fraction were multiplied by 10.

(b) £1 buys five 20p booklets.
So £400 buys 5 × 400 booklets, or 2000 booklets.

> (a) How many halves are there in 4?
>
> (b) Evaluate $4 \div \frac{1}{2}$.

(a) 8   (b) 8

A division is an answer to a question of the type, 'How many times is one number contained in another number?'

E X E R C I S E   2

1 29   **2** 85   **3** 16

4 16   **5** 200   **6** 300

7 £6 × 3 = £18. The total cost is 3p less than this, i.e. £17·97.

6.3   About right

> How can you check the answer to:
>
> (a) a subtraction;   (b) a division?

(a) Adding your answer to the number you subtracted should give the other number.

(b) Multiplying your answer by the number you divided by should give the other number.

The **inverse** of subtraction is addition.
The **inverse** of division is multiplication.

> Use your calculator to work out the answer correct to 3 significant figures.

The answer is 264   (to 3 s.f.).

EXERCISE   3

1   The value is a little more than $3 \times 4 \times 4 = 48$. To 1 significant figure it is 50.

2   The fuel costs nearly £2·50 a gallon, so £10 buys 4 gallons and £30 buys 12 gallons.
12 gallons takes me 12×32 or 384 miles.
So £30 takes me a **little** more than 384 miles. It will not be enough for a 400 mile journey.

3   The answer is roughly $(6 \times 10) \div 4 = 60 \div 4 = 15$.

4   Fiona's answer should be roughly $5 \times 400 = 2000$.

5   The plants cost more than $18 \times £5 = £90$.
$35 \times £2·13$ is not much more than $35 \times £2 = £70$.
The secretary is not asking for enough.

6   To convert an annual salary to a weekly wage you need to divide by 52. The result of doubling and then dividing by 100 is to divide by 50. This therefore gives a good estimate of the weekly wage.

6.4   What is the answer?

EXERCISE   4

1   About 576 seconds or 9 minutes 36 seconds. A tolerance of about 6 seconds should be allowed.

2 $366 \times 24 \times 60 \times 60 = 3.16224 \times 10^7$ This answer is exact!

3   22 yards $= \frac{22}{1760} = 0.0125$ mile
The ball is in the air for:

$$\frac{0.0125}{100} = 0.000125 \text{ hour}$$

i.e. $0.000125 \times 3600 = 0.45$ second

[The accuracy of this answer depends upon precisely where the bowler releases the ball and also depends upon the accuracy of the device used to measure the ball's speed.]

4   The length is 30 cm; the breadth is 21 cm.

(a) $30 \times 21 = 630$

(b) The greatest area is $30.5 \times 21.5 = 655.75 \text{ cm}^2$.
The least area is $29.5 \times 20.5 = 604.75 \text{ cm}^2$.

(c) A sensible value is 630 cm^2 with a tolerance of 26 cm^2 either way.